*Hawaiian
Flowers &
Flowering Trees*

By the same authors:
  The Modern Tropical Garden
  Hawaiian Flowers

Hawaiian Flowers & Flowering Trees: A Guide to Tropical & Semitropical Flora

by Loraine E. Kuck
and Richard C. Tongg

CHARLES E. TUTTLE COMPANY
Rutland, Vermont & Tokyo, Japan

Representatives

For Continental Europe:
BOXERBOOKS, INC., *Zurich*

For the British Isles:
PRENTICE-HALL INTERNATIONAL, INC., *London*

For Australasia:
PAUL FLESCH & CO., PTY. LTD., *Melbourne*

For Canada:
M. G. HURTIG LTD., *Edmonton*

Published by the Charles E. Tuttle Company, Inc.
of Rutland, Vermont & Tokyo, Japan
with editorial offices at
Suido 1-chome, 2-6, Bunkyo-ku, Tokyo

Library of Congress Catalog
Card No. 58-7494

Standard Book No. 8048 0227-0

First popular edition, 1960
Ninth printing, 1969

Illustrations by Frank Yasutaro Oda, Charles Taketa
and Masakazu Kuwata; Layout by Mary Goto Radner

PRINTED IN JAPAN

Contents

Publisher's Note   vii

Preface   ix

Chapter One: *Hawaii's Flowers*   1

Chapter Two: *Blossoming Trees*   21

Chapter Three: *Flowering Vines*   55

Chapter Four: *Tropical Shrubs*   87

Chapter Five: *Tropicalia*   127

Index   153

Publisher's Note
to the Popular Edition

THE CORDIAL reception given this book in its earlier clothbound edition indicated an interest well beyond the scope that the title appeared to suggest. Since, as the authors point out, "every flower and plant we see in Hawaii is a traveler or the descendant of a traveler," the book has been found to serve admirably as a guide to floral beauty found in many tropical and semitropical areas. In fact, the countries and regions of origin of the brilliant migrants pictured here make a truly cosmopolitan list that includes Africa, Argentina, Asia Minor, Australia, Bolivia, Brazil, Central America, Ceylon, China, Colombia, the East Indies, Fiji, Guatemala, Guiana, the Himalayas, India, Japan, Java, Madagascar, Malaya, the Mascarene Islands, Mexico, the Philippines, Polynesia, Rhodesia, Tahiti, and the West Indies.

Even more interestingly, the success with which so many flowers and flowering trees have been transplanted from one area of the tropics and the subtropics to another is a decided encouragement to gardeners and flower lovers of these regions to add to the splendor of their own collections. It is therefore hoped that this popular edition of the book will serve as a guide not only to the flowers and flowering trees already found in these regions but also to the assembling of an even more impressive display of floral beauty.

Preface

THE PURPOSE of this book is to answer the eternal question of visitors to the tropics: "What flower is that?" The wealth of flowering trees, vines, and shrubs, all unfamiliar to the usual visitor, arouses a great desire to know more about them.

In this book we have endeavored to give a quick answer to this question through pictures. The unknown flower can be identified by its portrait, then its name and other facts about it can be learned from the accompanying caption and text. Each caption shows first the common name or names by which the plant is known, then its scientific name, the family to which it belongs, and its place of origin. The caption is then followed by a text giving a description of the plant and other details which we feel to be significant or, sometimes, simply interesting.

This method was followed in our earlier work, *Hawaiian Flowers,* first published in 1943. In that book the flower pictures were grouped into a comparatively few plates. In the present book, almost every flower has been given an individual page, which of course allows each one to be larger, clearer, and more attractive.

The three artists who have worked on these paintings are Frank Y. Oda, Charles Taketa, and Masakazu Kuwata. The page layouts are the work of Mary Goto Radner. To these friends we express our appreciation for their special talents and for their painstaking interest and care.

A new chapter has been added in this book to tell the story of the Hawaiian flora. The background of both the plants seen in gardens and the remarkable native flora is covered. We believe the story of these plants, which have all crossed two thousand miles of water, will add depth and understanding to an appreciation of island floral beauty. The earlier text has been brought up to date and most of it rewritten.

LORAINE E. KUCK
RICHARD C. TONGG

Honolulu, 1958

Chapter One

Hawaii's Flowers

EVERY flower and plant we see in Hawaii is a traveler or the descendant of a traveler. Each kind must have crossed at least two thousand miles of salt water to get to these islands. For the Hawaiian chain has always been an island group, since it was formed. No land bridges ever existed to the continents along which plants and animals could make their way.

The chain rose in the center of the ocean as boiling masses of lava. Geologists tell us a great crack or weakness exists in the earth's crust in the central Pacific region, which has encouraged volcanic activity along its length. The activity seems to have begun at the northwest end, perhaps with the island of Midway, and has moved slowly along the crack, building up underwater mountain peaks as it went. Some of these rose above the ocean to form islands. Such activity still continues periodically on the Big Island of Hawaii.

Plants which became established here had to reach the islands through the air, on water, or aboard some carrier. Today, new arrivals are still coming in by airplane. The briefness of present-day flights makes it possible for delicate plants, which could never otherwise withstand the passage, to be brought from far places. Each year sees many new plants imported, both for ornamental and commercial experimentation.

The greater part of all the plants and trees ordinarily seen in Hawaiian gardens, fields, and hillsides was brought here in modern ships within the last hundred years. They came as planned introductions or as undetected weeds. Over a large part of the islands these aggressive foreigners have now crowded out most of the natives.

Thus the brilliant flowering trees and shrubs, the lush herbaceous tropicals, and the strange exotic blossoms in Hawaiian gardens are the choice gleanings from all the world. They have come from jungles and deserts, from monsoon lands, and from other ocean islands. Probably no other tropical area, even Florida, has, as yet, such a large and spreading collection. In Hawaii's group, a large number have come from the lands of the East, for new residents brought their cherished favorites with them. South China, in particular, with its congenially similar climate, has contributed many. In general, islanders have long delighted to gather new plants on their travels, or to study foreign catalogs and send for enticing novelties.

In the days of slow sailing ships, when such introductions were in their early stages, plants were transported in small portable greenhouses, called wardian cases, set up on the decks of ships. These glassed-in boxes were ingeniously contrived to protect the plants from salt spray, while giving them enough air, and to be virtually self-watering. The plants could live and grow in them for months with very little attention.

Among the plants commonly seen in Hawaii are a few that were brought before the days of modern ships. These rode as valued cargo in the great double sailing canoes of the Polynesian voyagers—the people who were the first to discover and settle the Hawaiian Islands. Such settlers brought with them the plants they would need in their new homes. About twenty-four such plants are believed to have come in this way.[1] They include the coconut, breadfruit, banana, bamboo, *kukui*, or candlenut tree (for its oily nuts), the hau tree (to provide canoe outriggers from its curved branches), the milo tree (for making flavorless wooden poi bowls), and the paper mulberry (for making tapa cloth). They also brought taro, sweet potatoes, yams, the ti plant, sugar cane, wild ginger, and the bottle gourd.[2, 3]

However, in Hawaii's high mountains and its hidden valleys there still grow the native plants whose ancestors arrived by even earlier conveyances than the canoes. These ancestors were the hitchhikers. As seeds, they became stuck to the feathers and feet of birds and traveled long distances with them. Or they might have become attached to logs and trees which were washed up on the shore by ocean currents.

Others of the earliest plant travelers arrived quite alone, not as riders. A few, able to withstand salt water, may have floated in on ocean currents. Others, the tiny dustlike spores of ferns and some tree seeds, were so fine and light they could be whirled into the upper atmosphere by storms and then float along for thousands of miles before descending to earth. Most of those which made the trip and landed on the islands probably failed to find a suitable growing place. But some did, as the observed facts prove.

One might think that a seed stuck to a bird's feather or floating through the upper atmosphere would have only a long, long chance of actually traveling any such distance and, on coming down, lodging in a place where it could grow and reproduce its kind. The chances, undoubtedly were very long. But listen to the estimate of Dr. F. R. Fosberg on the frequency of such chance occurrences.

"Of seed plants," he says, "one successful arrival and establishment every 20,000 to 30,000 years could account for the (island) flora."[4] A period of twenty thousand years does not seem impossibly long in which *one* such successful incident might have taken place!

This estimate is based on the assumption that five to ten million years have passed since the first of the Hawaiian island

3

chain boiled above the ocean's surface. It might have been Kure (Ocean Island), or Midway, or Pearl and Hermes Reef. These islands and the others along the chain may once have become fairly high land masses, but eventually they were eroded to sea level and became atolls, sand islets, or shoals. At the same time other islands down the chain were growing up. We see this process still going on from Kauai to Hawaii, Kauai being the oldest and Hawaii the youngest in the main group. It is assumed that plants which secured a foothold on one island might, with *comparatively* little trouble, have gained the next and the next, until the overall effect of successive arrivals became cumulative.

On the results of such haphazard methods of introduction Dr. Fosberg further comments: "It (the Hawaiian flora) is exactly the type that might be expected to be descended from a random aggregation of chance waifs carried over the seas by a combination of such factors as storms, currents and birds." The list of plant groups from which the native Hawaiian flora has descended shows large gaps when compared to the list of all the world's plant groups. The missing groups are the ones which did not succeed in getting an ancestral member across the seas to the islands.

In all the millions of years before the Polynesians finally touched these islands (which was probably only a thousand years ago) it is estimated that the safe arrival and establishment of some four hundred ancestors would account for the native species. The exact estimates are 272 ancestors of flowering plants and 135 for ferns. (The high proportion of ferns only indicates that their tiny, light spores get around more easily than do heavier seeds.)

But even the travels of the original ancestors may not be the most interesting part of the story of Hawaii's native plants. Although some 272 ancestral floral kinds made successful landings without man's help, by the time the scientists got around to counting and classifying the island species, about a hundred years ago, it was found there were at least 1,792 different kinds. (Subsequent discoveries indicate that this number may well be low.[5]) Of these, only 4.6 per cent are plants found elsewhere. About 94.4 per cent are plants *not* found elsewhere in the world. These are the true natives, or endemic species which came into existence right here. This percentage of endemism is the highest known anywhere.

It is, of course, also the result of the islands' isolation. In a large area, like a continent, where many plants of one kind are constantly crossbreeding, the tendency is to maintain a common type by suppressing individual variations through common dominance. But where every plant in a small group is the descendant of a single individual, inbreeding encourages any new or differing tendencies the single individual may have possessed. And through the selective influence of environment new species are more easily developed.

Hawaii's endemic species have thus come into existence by the usual process of variation and self-selection through survival. The 94.4 per cent of endemic plants have developed from the earlier arrivals. The 4.6 per cent of indigenous plants are probably the late arrivals, those which have not yet had time to change.

A few of Hawaii's new species may have arisen through mutation, that is, through the occurrence of a single variation so large and heritable that it produced a new species in a single generation. But among the small variations (and it has been said that "variation is the most invariable thing in nature") some particular ones would make its possessor a little better fitted to survive under the special conditions in which it grew. These individuals lived to pass on such favorable characteristics to their offspring, and, as this process continued, the descendants eventually came to have quite different characteristics. In other words, a new species gradually came into existence.

Out of this process of selection based on environment has come another peculiarity of Hawaii's native flora, that is, its high dependence on local conditions. A great many (although not all) of the native species grow only in quite small areas. Sometimes they are found only on a single island, or even in a single valley or isolated ledge. And often these species cannot be made to grow anywhere else, even in situations which seem almost identical. On the other hand, a few have spread widely and have succeeded in crossing rugged mountains, desert-like dry areas, and strong ocean currents to reach another island. That comparatively few do this is shown by the fact that the older island of Kauai has a much greater number of native plants than does the young island of Hawaii.[1]

The demand for highly specialized conditions of growth on the part of so many native island plants is one of the main reasons why they are not more often seen in island gardens. Most of them simply cannot be made to grow anywhere except in their limited native areas. A major reason is found in the fact that most gardens are located fairly close to the seashore where the climate is quite different from the cool dampness of the mountains. But even in mountain gardens many native plants will not tolerate comparatively slight differences in soil and climate.

Still another reason why so few native plants are seen in Hawaiian gardens is that very few of them can be regarded as interesting garden material. While they are of absorbing interest to the botanist, most are not showy and only a few have bright flowers. The early Hawaiians, for example, had few outstanding flower leis. One came from the blossoms of the red lehua tree, another was made by stringing together the tiny yellow flowers of the ilima. The yellow ginger furnished a third. Even these were not true natives.

Hawaiian gardens do make use of some local plants, mostly those which grow in the shore areas. But the majority of these also are not true natives of Hawaii but are found in other parts of the Pacific. The coconut palm, of course, is the first to come to mind among such plants. Other trees are the hala, hau, milo, kou, the tree ferns, and the beach naupaka, a shrub. These are described in the pages immediately following.

To find real native plants of Hawaii growing wild, one must go to the higher mountain slopes or to the curious bogs found on the summits of some Hawaiian mountains. Certain natives may be found in both sections of the Hawaii National Park, that on Hawaii and that on Maui, because they are protected. A really spectacular native is the silver sword *(Argyroxiphium sandwicense* DC), a sort of sunflower. This pushes up its stalk and leaves, covered with protective silver-colored hairs, among the dry lava near the top of Haleakala. It will not grow in apparently more favorable situations.

But as said earlier, the plants and flowers seen mostly in island gardens are imports from all the world. Newcomers sometimes wonder why, among these, more plants from the temperate zone are not found. It would seem they should thrive in the mild climate. But they do not. The reason is that most "temperate zone" plants are conditioned to seasons of cold or heat or dryness which bring a rest period, and unless they have such conditions which allow them to rest, they do not grow well, if at all. Plants imported from other tropical or mild climates, however, are readily established and many now live happily together—just as do the people from many different lands who have come here also.

References and Bibliography

1. Hillebrand, William. *Flora of the Hawaiian Islands.* 1888.
2. Bryan, E. H. Jr. *The Hawaiian Chain.* Bishop Museum Press, 1954.

7

3. Neal, Marie C. *In Gardens of Hawaii*. Bishop Museum Special Publication, 1948.
4. For Fosberg, see: Zimmerman, E. C. *Insects of Hawaii*, Vol. I. University of Hawaii Press, 1948.
5. Degener, Otto. *Ferns and Flowering Plants of Hawaii National Park*. Honolulu, 1930.
6. Degener, Otto. *Flora Hawaiiensis*. 1946.
7. Rock, J. F. *Leguminous Plants of Hawaii*. 1920 : and other writings.

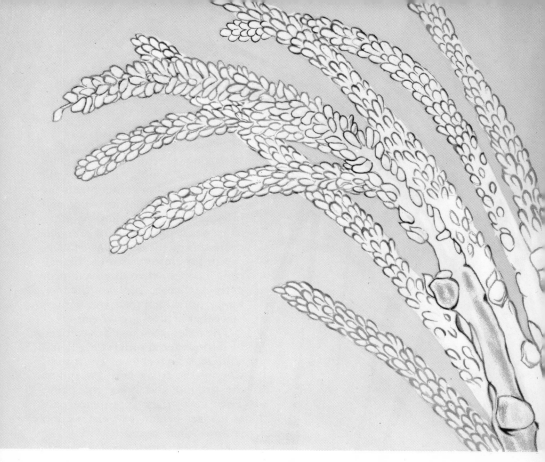

Coconut

Cocos nucifera Linnaeus
Palm family
Tropical cosmopolitan

THE GRACEFUL coconut palm needs no description with its slender, leaning trunk and tuft of luxuriant feather-type leaves. Some leaves may be eighteen feet long. The coconut blossom, however, is not often seen because it comes out among the leaves and is usually many feet above the ground. It must be cut and brought down to be examined. The bud emerges as a pointed club, several inches across and two or more feet long. It is enclosed in a tough woody sheath which splits and falls off. The fountaining flower which emerges suggests an intricate piece of ivory carving, all parts being hard and white. It is composed of many branches which hold small knobs near their bases. These are the future coconuts. The outer ends of the branches are lined with double rows of grainlike teeth, which are the staminate flowers. This flower may develop into a bunch of as many as forty coconuts.

9

THE HALA is a small tree or shrub which suggests a palm, with long, narrow, pointed leaves which are tough, fibrous, and usually spiny. On young plants the leaves grow from the trunk and branches in ascending spirals, hence the name screwpine. On older specimens the leaves have fallen, except for clusters near the branch ends. Leaves, when dried and properly prepared, become the *lauhala,* from which mats and numerous other articles are woven.

The older trees are characterized by curious aerial roots straight and stiltlike, which emerge from partway up the trunk and descend to the ground and brace the plant. They make their appearance only as the tree becomes top heavy and requires their support.

Male and female trees are separate. On the female trees the fruit looks somewhat like a pineapple at the ends of the branches. It is made up of fibrous, shining sections, or drupes, which become deep yellow as they ripen, then separate and fall. A fruit lei is made by cutting these sections into short pieces and stringing them.

The male tree is called *hinano.* The flower is a drooping, whitish plume, made up of hundreds of tiny, yellow staminate flowers loaded with pollen. They grow on clustered, drooping stems partially enclosed in long, whitish bracts.

Hala or **Screwpine** .
Pandanus odoratissimus Linnaeus
Screwpine family
Polynesia and Malaya

10

Ilima

Sida fallax Walpers
Hibiscus family
Hawaii and Pacific

THE ILIMA is a low, sprawling, often scrubby, little shrub with woody branches. It is frequently seen growing wild in dry places but certain varieties may be cultivated in gardens, primarily for the purpose of providing flowers for leis. Leaves are small, blunt, bright green, and slightly scalloped. The flowers are solitary, or in twos or threes, scattered over the plant on short stems. They resemble a small hibiscus, about an inch across, with five crepy petals and a group of stamens in the center. Flower colors range from pale yellow through orange to brown. These are strung into leis by threading them through the center.

They were formerly known as royal leis, since only chiefs were allowed to wear them. Today the ilima is regarded as the special flower of the island of Oahu.

Kukui or
Candlenut Tree

Aleurites moluccana (L) Willdenow
Splurge family
Malaysia and Polynesia

GROVES of the kukui tree are easily seen on Hawaiian hillsides because of their light foliage. The trees tend to cluster in protected ravines where, seen from below, they make blotches of greyish green. They will grow down to sea level, however, and are often used in gardens.

The leaves of this tree vary greatly. One type has pointed lobes, another has its lobes flattened into almost regular form. They are covered with a greyish down, which is heaviest on the underside. The white flowers are very small and have five petals. They grow in soft, massed clusters, the male and female flowers appearing separately on the same tree. The staminate flowers are on the upper branches, the pistillate flowers lower down. Sometimes the fruit and flower hang on at the same time.

The round, green fruit contains a nut, which was very useful to the early Hawaiians. Containing a high percentage of oil, it was used to make a torch by stringing it on the midrib of a coconut leaf. When roasted the nut is edible and has a strong purgative action.

12

Mountain or Malay Apple
Eugenia malaccensis Linnaeus
Myrtle family
India and Malaya

RED FLOWERS that grow on short stems directly from the trunk and main branches of the tree make the mountain apple conspicuous during winter and spring. The tufts of red stamens are the most noticeable part of the flower, but short, rounded petals of the same color inclose them.

The fruit, which begins to ripen in June, suggests in color and shape a small red and pinkish apple. The skin is very thin and waxen, the flesh white, crisp, and juicy. Its flavor is not distinctive. There is a large brown seed in the center.

In favorable locations the tree attains fifty feet in height, with smooth, dark green leaves. It grows wild in protected shady valleys where the rainfall is plentiful. This was one of the plants the early Hawaiians brought with them in their sailing canoes and was the only fruit they had before others were introduced by Europeans.

Maile
Alyxia olivaeformis Gaudichaud
Periwinkle family
Hawaii

THE MAILE (pronounced to rhyme with smiley) is a straggling shrub or vine which is a true native of Hawaii. It is almost never seen in gardens but grows wild in the cool, green depths of the middle and lower forest zones. Its leaves are smooth, leathery, and shining, about one and a half inches long. They come out usually in threes along the stem. In the leaf axils appear the small, yellowish flowers, most often, also in threes. These are followed by tiny, black fruits.

The maile is the great traditional lei plant of Hawaii, formerly worn by chief and commoner alike. The lei was made by twining several stems together. It was not closed into a wreath but left open. Its most appealing characteristic is a faint woodsy scent of anise noticed when the leaves begin to dry.

Ohia Lehua

Metrosideros collina var. *polymorpha*
  (Gaud.) Rock
Myrtle family
Polynesia

THIS TREE grows well only under the cool conditions of the higher slopes of the islands, such as those which prevail in the Hawaii National Park on the Big Island. There it becomes one of the largest and finest of Hawaiian trees, attaining a hundred feet. The species is extremely variable, however, so that the plant is often seen only as a shrub.

Its foliage varies also, but usually is small, rounded or blunt, greyish, and close growing. The flowers appear principally as a tuft of red stamens, although they have small petals. Occasionally pink, yellow, or creamy white variations occur. The flowers were used for one of the most popular of the early leis. Held to be sacred to Pele, goddess of the volcano, it was believed that she would cause rain to fall on those who picked them without first making her a proper offering. The ohia wood is hard, dark, and beautiful and is much used for fine cabinet work, carvings, and floors.

15

Hau Tree

Hibiscus tiliaceus Linnaeus
Hibiscus family
Tropical cosmopolitan

A TREE found on Pacific beaches has the unusual habit of creeping and twisting along the ground instead of growing upright. It is called the hau (pronounced how) and is a true hibiscus. In its native state its long sinuous branches interlock and eventually form jungles too thick to penetrate. In gardens, this mass of branches is sometimes trained to grow over an arborlike framework, resulting in a shelter which is called a *hau lanai*. Some very old garden trees, used this way, have developed trunks which are two or more feet thick and are extremely picturesque in their irregularity. The native Hawaiians used the curved branches of this tree to make the outriggers for their canoes.

The flower has the typical hibiscus form, with five crepy petals and a central column. It is about three inches across. The color is a clear, bright yellow when the flower first opens, but as it grows older the color changes to an apricot hue, and when it finally falls it is dark red. The leaves are heart-shaped or rounded, green, and leathery, with whitish hairs beneath.

Milo Tree
Thespesia populnea (L) Solander
Hibiscus family
Tropical Orient and Pacific
(no illustration)

AN UPRIGHT tree with heart-shaped leaves and flowers like small, yellow hibiscus blossoms is the milo. It is closely related to the true hibiscus. The tree grows along the shore of the Hawaiian and other Pacific islands where it is much used for shade. The five-petaled flowers open to a bell shape. They are a pale yellow color when fresh, with a dark red spot near the base, very similar to the hau blossom. As they fade, they turn to a purplish pink. The flower is followed by a five-parted cap-sule, which turns brown and hangs on the tree a long time. The wood of this tree was much used by the early Hawaiians to make food bowls, because it was almost free from flavor.

Kamani Tree
Calophyllum inophyllum Linnaeus
Mangosteen family
India and the Pacific
(no illustration)

AN ATTRACTIVE tree found growing along the shore has large, thick, leathery leaves, very smooth and shining, and clusters of fragrant, waxy, white flowers. The latter have four to eight petals and four sepals around a central mass of golden stamens and a red pistil. Each is about an inch across.

The clusters may contain a dozen or more flowers. The leaves are leathery, blunt, and oval with many fine, parallel side veins. The tree may attain sixty feet and has a rough, grey bark. Growing in windy areas, it is often picturesque-ly misshapen. It bears a small, green fruit, which produces an oil much used by the Hawaiians. This plant is among those which it is believed they brought with them to Hawaii.

Breadfruit
Artocarpus incisus (Thunb.) Lin-naeus fils
Fig family
Malaysia
(no illustration)

THE TERM "breadfruit" is rather misleading, for the fruit of this tree, when cooked, is more like a sweet potato than like bread. The tree is very picturesque, with large tropical leaves. It attains about forty feet on the average but may be higher. Each bright green leaf is about three feet long and is deeply cut into rounded lobes. The staminate flowers grow in an up-right, yellowish green cylinder at the branch tips. The pistillate flowers form a large ball just be-low. The latter develops into the fruit, a round, green globe, rough on the surface, which may become eight inches in diameter. When ripe it is brownish. This fruit is one of the staples of diet in the South Seas.

17

Beach Naupaka

Scaevola frutescens (Mill.) Krause,
var. *sericea* Merr
Naupaka family
Hawaii

A SHRUB which has proved of great use in Hawaiian seaside gardens, where salt spray often kills other plants, is the naupaka. It grows wild on dry, island beaches where its fresh, soft, bright green leaves, almost succulent in quality, are conspicuous. The commonly seen plant is a native Hawaiian variety, of the type species which grows in other parts of the Pacific. The naupaka plant may become a rounded, green mound, ten feet high, but is usually smaller. It is extensively used for informal hedges. The thick, silky leaves are broader at the tip, slightly notched and narrow toward the leaf stem. The small, fragrant, white flowers are curiously shaped, in that half the flower appears to have been torn away. Small, white berries follow the flowers.

Koa Tree

Acacia koa Gray
Legume, mimosa subfamily
Hawaii
(no illustration)

THIS IS Hawaii's largest and finest native tree, growing sometimes to over a hundred feet. It has a fine straight trunk and is the tree from which the native canoes were made. As the tree grows only in the cooler mountain areas, the great logs were pulled down to the ocean by the whole village after they had been partially hollowed out.

The koa is marked by its sickle-shaped foliage which is a greyish green in color. These are not true leaves, however, but modified leaf stems. True leaves, seen in seedlings or sometimes on young growth, are doubly compound. The koa blossoms are inconspicuous, pale yellow balls of stamens, similar to those seen on other species of acacia.

The Ti Plant
Cordyline terminalis (L) Kunth
Lily family
Tropical Asia and the Pacific

THE GREEN-LEAVED ti (pronounced tee) grows wild and very abundantly in the lower wet forests of Hawaii and is often used in shady gardens as a hedge or background plant. It is a tall stalk, usually unbranched, which may sometimes become twelve feet high. Its base is woody. The leaves appear in a tuft near the top. They are blade-shaped, about four inches wide, and up to three feet long. Thick, glossy, and strong, they do not wilt quickly, so they proved useful to the early Hawaiians for many purposes and are still much used even today. Shredded, they make the skirt of the hula dancer or they may cover the table at which native feasts are served.

In winter the flower stalk emerges from among the leaves and produces a many-branched cluster. It holds hundreds of tiny, white flowers, which are really minute lilies. Sepals are often mauve or pinkish, so the effect of the cluster may be pinkish grey or cream.

Colored Tis

The ti plant varies greatly, many forms having colored foliage and variously shaped leaves. The leaf colors are mostly tones of red or greenish white, ranging from maroon to bright pink, while some have bronze or golden hues. The flowers of the colored ti are cerise pink. They usually produce clusters of small, red berries, in contrast to the green form of the plant, which seldom fruits.

Chapter Two

Blossoming Trees

HAWAII'S most impressive floral displays occur when the flowering trees line the streets or fill the gardens. The effect of these trees often rivals, in the masses of their flowers, the fruit trees of the mainland. But they possess colorings of tropical brilliance which have no rivals outside of warm countries. Moreover, instead of blooming for a few brief days, or at most, weeks, many of these continue in flower for months at a time. A few are everblooming.

About the middle of June there is a period when the display is at its best. At this time all the "shower" trees are out, the early ones still lingering, the later ones coming on. It is, the time also when the red of the royal poinciana, the blue of the jacaranda, and the pink and white of plumeria and bauhinia add their hues to the galaxy. Flowers from all the world's tropics have been assembled for this pageant of the blooming trees. It is one of Hawaii's most characteristic beauties.

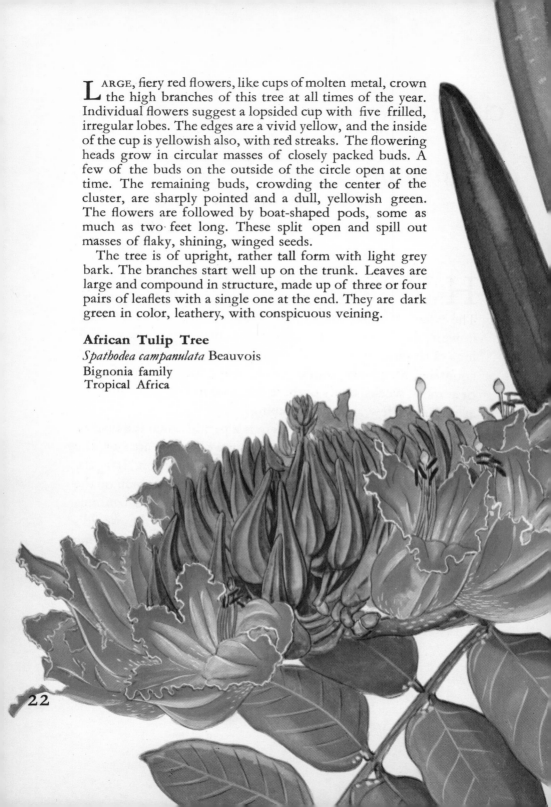

L ARGE, fiery red flowers, like cups of molten metal, crown the high branches of this tree at all times of the year. Individual flowers suggest a lopsided cup with five frilled, irregular lobes. The edges are a vivid yellow, and the inside of the cup is yellowish also, with red streaks. The flowering heads grow in circular masses of closely packed buds. A few of the buds on the outside of the circle open at one time. The remaining buds, crowding the center of the cluster, are sharply pointed and a dull, yellowish green. The flowers are followed by boat-shaped pods, some as much as two feet long. These split open and spill out masses of flaky, shining, winged seeds.

The tree is of upright, rather tall form with light grey bark. The branches start well up on the trunk. Leaves are large and compound in structure, made up of three or four pairs of leaflets with a single one at the end. They are dark green in color, leathery, with conspicuous veining.

African Tulip Tree
Spathodea campanulata Beauvois
Bignonia family
Tropical Africa

22

Dombeya

Dombeya wallichii Benthan and Hooker
Cocoa family
Madagascar

Many heavy, pendant balls of pale pink flowers make a small dombeya tree rather a breath-taking sight if one stands so as to look up into it. The flowers are not so plainly seen from the side, since the foliage is very heavy. Each flower-head, hanging at the end of a long, downy pedicel, is made up of many dainty pink florets, each with five petals and the stamens united to form a short tube in the center. They bloom during the autumn and winter and are at their best about December. When they fade, they do not fall off, so the masses of dried, brown bloom are visible for a long time.

The leaves are big and velvety, somewhat angularly heart-shaped. The tree reaches about thirty feet and is vigorous and upright.

23

Royal Poinciana or Flamboyant

Delonix regia (Bojer) Rafinesque
Legume, senna subfamily
Madagascar

OF ALL Hawaii's flowering trees, the royal poinciana is easily the most conspicuous for sheer color and brightness. While it is often almost a solid mass of red, it is not merely colorful but a graceful and picturesque tree. Its form is a flat umbrella in the smaller specimens, or a dome of long sweeping curves in the larger ones, the branches having been pulled down by the weight of its heavy pods.

The tree may become forty feet high, if growing under favorable conditions, but if the roots are cramped it remains small. Although bare for a short time in winter, some trees begin to bloom early in spring, while others wait until late summer to open. June is the month when most of them are in flower.

Individual poinciana flowers, difficult to distinguish in the masses of bloom, have five petals. One of these, on the flag red trees, is white. It is yellow on trees tending toward orange scarlet coloring. These light touches give a piquant effect to the mass of color. Very heavy, long, brown pods filled with seeds, hang on the tree for months after blooming.

The flowers usually appear on the bare tree before the new foliage comes out, but in a short time the leaves appear, and for some weeks the green and red colorings remain together. The leaves are fernlike, doubly compound in form, with very small leaflets.

Yellow Poinciana
Peltophorum inerme Roxburgh
Legume family
Malaya

A LARGE tree with many upright spikes of small, deep yellow flowers, bright against the greenery of fine-cut leaves, is called yellow poinciana because the individual flowers suggest those of the related royal poinciana. The tree is also characterized by masses of small, reddish brown pods. The flower buds are small and round and are covered with velvety, brown down. This same down also covers the young growth and the midribs of the leaves. Individual flowers have five crepy petals of about equal size. The large, triangular heads of bloom are made up of smaller clusters. The reddish brown pods are thin and flat and hold three or four seeds. They remain on the tree for a long time, often being seen at the same time as the flowers.

The leaves are doubly compound with many small, rounded leaflets. The tree is always green. It may grow to fifty feet in upright form.

Orchid Tree or Bauhinia
Bauhinia variegata var. *candida* Linnaeus
Legume, senna subfamily
India

THE MOST conspicuous white-flowering tree of early spring in Hawaii is the orchid tree. Although the flower suggests a small orchid blossom, the plant is not related to the orchids in any way. The paper white petals of the blossoms are lightly veined in green. Four petals are of similar form, the fifth is larger and broader. The projecting green pistil develops into a pod after the flowers fade. These pods hang on the tree for a long time.

The name orchid tree seems even more applicable to the lavender-flowered type of this species. These trees are not so conspicuous as the white, but their individual flowers look even more like orchids, due to their coloring. The fifth petal is broadly stained with a deeper purplish rose than the others. Four white stamens grow from the center.

Both become small trees, twenty feet high. Their leaves have the curious double lobes, suggesting a green moth, which are characteristic of the bauhinias. Prominent veins radiate from the point where the stem joins the blade.

Bombax

Bombax ellipticum Humboldt, Bon-
pland, and Kunth
Bombax family
Mexico

A BOMBAX tree growing in the
Queen's Hospital grounds in
Honolulu presents such a striking
appearance when in bloom that it
has become a regular object of
interest. The flowers appear re-
gularly in March on the bare tree,
a few at a time, suggesting a bunch
of pink egret plumes. The bud,
growing upright on the bare
branch, is like a stubby cigar, rising from the calyx, as from the cup
of an acorn. The bud splits into
five parts, which peel backward
like a banana and curl into spirals.
These are the petals, purplish
brown outside, silky white within.
The conspicuous part of the flower
is the great pompon of pink
stamens, an exploding rocket of
color. They are about five inches
long.

Except when in bloom, the tree
is inconspicuous with its grey
bark, and foliage made up of five
large, radiating leaflets. The tree is
bare for several months.

27

Colvillea

Colvillea racemosa Bojer
Legume family
Madagascar

IN LATE October and November
when most of the flowering trees
are gone, the colvillea breaks into
sudden spectacular bloom. Tre-
mendous bunches of red orange
buds appear at the tips of the
branches, suggesting gigantic tas-
sels. On closer inspection they
seem more like great bunches of
orange velvet grapes, for the buds
are round and covered with a thick
velvety calyx. As many as two
hundred of these buds may be
crowded in one bunch, and several
bunches hang at the tip of each
branch.

Daily a few buds at the head
split open to reveal the true flower.
Its general form is that of a pea
blossom with small, red orange
petals. A large tuft of bright
yellow stamens projects from the
center. Fallen flowers cover the
ground with an orange carpet.
Some of the flowers are followed
by seed pods.

The tree suggests its relative, the
poinciana. in form and in its large,
compound leaves made up of many
tiny leaflets.

Crepe Myrtle Tree
Lagerstroemia speciosa Persoon
Crepe myrtle family
India

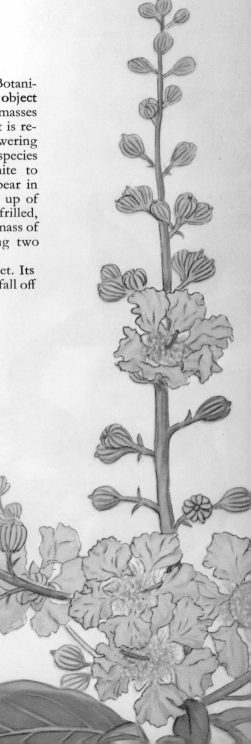

A LAVENDER-FLOWERING tree in Foster Botanical Garden becomes a conspicuous object during the summer when it is covered with masses of flowers. As a species of crepe myrtle, it is related to the commoner pink- or white-flowering shrub of that name. Flowers of this large species may vary considerably in hue, from white to pink or deep lavender. These flowers appear in large, loose, upright heads. Each is made up of six or more petals, which are extremely frilled, ruffled, and crepy. They surround a large mass of yellow stamens, the flower altogether being two inches or more across.

The tree may grow to fifty or sixty feet. Its leaves are rather long and pointed and fall off once a year in late winter.

Christmas Berry Tree
Schinus terebinthifolius Raddi
Mango family
Brazil

HAWAII uses the lasting, dry, red berries of this small tree for its Christmas decorations, for at that season the female trees are usually loaded with them. It is a close relative of the California pepper tree and like that has a pungent peppery smell. Unlike the pepper, however, its branches are not pendant, but rangy, and its leaves are dark green. The five to nine leaflets are each several inches long. In older specimens the tree assumes very picturesque gnarled and twisted forms, but young trees are more like shrubs. The small flowers generally appear in summer in inconspicuous greenish yellow clusters.

Angel's Trumpet

Datura candida (Pers) Pasquale
Tomato family
Tropical America

A CONSPICUOUS small tree with large, white, trumpet-shaped flowers hanging over it always attracts attention. Perhaps its name of angel's trumpet is inevitable. Each flower hangs like a bell. It is about ten inches long, with five thin segments each coming to a twisted point, and with an exotic scent of musk. The calyx enwrapping the end of the tube is a single lobe, split and somewhat pointed.

The tree averages about fifteen feet or less with light-colored bark. Its wood is very brittle. The large leaves are greyish green, thick and velvety, and about sixteen inches long.

31

Potato Tree

Solanum macranthum Hortorum
Tomato family
Brazil

RICH PURPLE blue blossoms appear in small clusters near the ends of the branches on this tree. Each is about two inches in diameter, its five segments joined to give it the form of a five-sided star. The flower begins to wither as soon as it is cut. The one illustrated had collapsed slightly, as seen, before the artist could finish his picture. The deep blue color fades in a day to a paler tone and then almost to white, making clusters of variegated flowers. Small, yellow berries sometimes follow the flowers. Spring is the flowering period.

Leaves of this medium-sized tree are about a foot long and irregularly lobed. The midrib and the branches carry sharp, hooked prickles. It is one of the few members of the tomato family which is a tree.

32

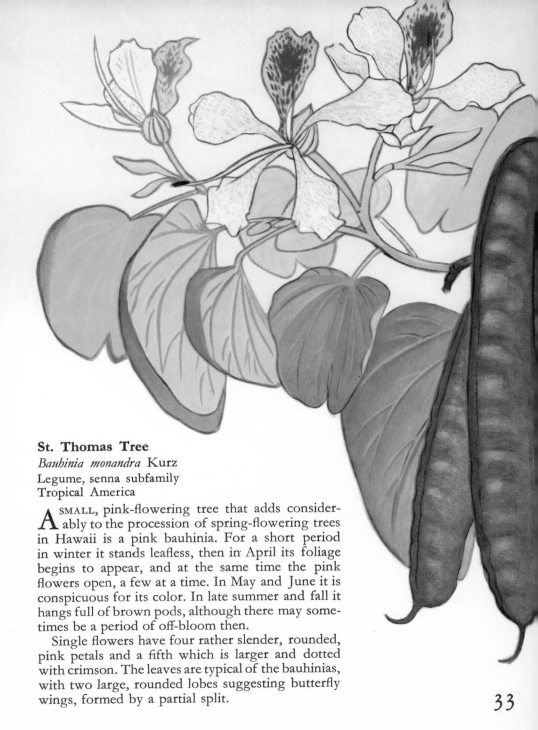

St. Thomas Tree
Bauhinia monandra Kurz
Legume, senna subfamily
Tropical America

A SMALL, pink-flowering tree that adds considerably to the procession of spring-flowering trees in Hawaii is a pink bauhinia. For a short period in winter it stands leafless, then in April its foliage begins to appear, and at the same time the pink flowers open, a few at a time. In May and June it is conspicuous for its color. In late summer and fall it hangs full of brown pods, although there may sometimes be a period of off-bloom then.

Single flowers have four rather slender, rounded, pink petals and a fifth which is larger and dotted with crimson. The leaves are typical of the bauhinias, with two large, rounded lobes suggesting butterfly wings, formed by a partial split.

33

Jacaranda

Jacaranda ovalifolia R. Brown
Bignonia family
Brazil

SINCE blue is the rarest color in the flower world, a tree which is a mass of blue is something to attract attention. Yet the rarity of the blue coloring in the jacaranda is but little more important than the beauty of the tree as a whole. It is a large tree, with light grey bark. Its foliage is almost as attractive as a fern, each leaf being in double-feather form with many tiny leaflets. They usually fall in late winter and early spring, so the tree is bare for a short time.

The flowers, which appear in large, loose clusters at the ends of the branches, are shaped like bells, with two lips, one with two lobes, the other with three. The color is a soft lavender blue. The blossoming period is erratic but is most often in spring. On individual trees, the blooming period is not long, but with varying times of bloom, a tree may usually be found in flower. The blossoms fall in masses, repeating their color on the ground like a reflection of the tree above. The seed pods are round and rather flat.

Pink Tecoma Tree

Tabebuia pentaphylla Hemsley or
Tecoma pentaphylla Jussieu
Bignonia family
Tropical America

A SMALL tree with a scattering, or sometimes masses, of pink, tubular flowers can be identified by its five-fingered foliage as the pink tecoma. The flower tube is white, the thin, spreading lobes a rosy pink, or sometimes lavender or white. These lobes are crepy, fluted, and irregular. They fall and frequently cover the ground with color. The blooming season is erratic, a few flowers being visible at almost any time, but there are seasons when they cover the tree.

The leaves have five leaflets of irregular size radiating from a common center. They are smooth and rather stiff, with short leafstalks. The tree is said to attain sixty feet in its native land but so far has only reached small to medium size in Hawaii.

35

Madre de Cacao
Gliricidia sepium (Jacquin) Steudel
Legume family
Tropical America

THIS TREE is notable for its early blooming, the masses of its pale pink flowers beginning to appear soon after Christmas. They go on more or less continuously through April. The effect of a blossoming tree, which usually is bare of foliage, is rather like that of an apple or peach tree, but individually, each flower is like a small, pink sweetpea. They grow on short flowering branches and are scentless. Many pods, which hang on the tree for a long time, follow the flowers.

While the tree is often bare when in bloom, the old foliage may have remained, or the new made its appearance. The leaves are compound, with ten or eleven leaflets. The tree grows to about twenty-five feet and when not in flower is rather undistinguished in appearance.

Cannon Ball Tree

Couroupita guianensis Aublet
Brazil nut family
Guiana

IN HONOLULU, a single specimen of this curiously flowering tree grows in Foster Botanical Garden, where it is much seen by visitors. Its strange, fragrant blossoms grow on short branches which push out of the main trunk of the tree. They have six thick, fleshy petals which are peach colored within, lemon yellow without. From the center of the flower droops a thick, hook-shaped part which is the staminal column, greatly modified. Its end is fringed with rose-colored stamens while a second set of stamens forms a flat, yellow mat in the center of the flower. A few of these blossoms may be seen at almost any time, but there is a season of plentiful bloom in autumn.

The Foster Garden tree seldom sets its fruits, but when it does these are round, hard-shelled balls, six to eight inches across, full of seeds. They give its common name to the tree. Its foliage is evergreen, the leaves pointed and up to a foot long.

37

Be-still Tree or
Yellow Oleander

Thevetia nereifolia Jussieu or *T. peruviana* (Persoon) K. Schumann
Periwinkle family
Tropical America

A SMALL tree holding a scattering of silky, trumpet-shaped, yellow flowers and narrow, shimmering, light green foliage is popularly called the be-still tree. There seems to be no good reason for this name. Its second name, yellow oleander, refers to the leaves which suggest those of the oleander (Nerium), thus accounting also for its specific botanical name of *nereifolia*. However, it is not related to the oleanders, and the name is misleading.

The flowers are a clear, satiny yellow with a delightful fragrance. They appear at all times of the year and hang individually over the tree. A less commonly seen kind is the variety *aurantiaca*. It has pale-orange-colored flowers.

All parts of this attractive tree are actively poisonous if eaten. The brown or black nut produces a powerful heart medicine.

Jetberry Tree

Ardisia solanacea Roxburgh
Myrsine family
Ceylon

NOTABLE for its large clusters of shining jet-black berries, each shaped like an old-fashioned shoe button, is the jetberry tree. The berries form in the autumn and for some time are an attractive red-dish pink color. They hang on the tree for many months. The small, pink or lavender flowers are rather inconspicuous when they come out in summer. The tree becomes about twenty feet tall in slender, upright form.

Its leaves are leathery and light green. The new growth at the tips of the branches is reddish.

39

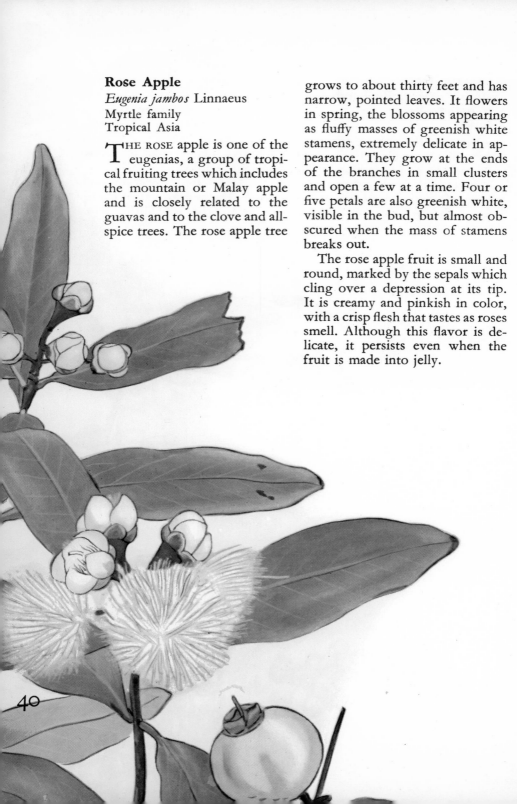

Rose Apple
Eugenia jambos Linnaeus
Myrtle family
Tropical Asia

THE ROSE apple is one of the eugenias, a group of tropical fruiting trees which includes the mountain or Malay apple and is closely related to the guavas and to the clove and allspice trees. The rose apple tree grows to about thirty feet and has narrow, pointed leaves. It flowers in spring, the blossoms appearing as fluffy masses of greenish white stamens, extremely delicate in appearance. They grow at the ends of the branches in small clusters and open a few at a time. Four or five petals are also greenish white, visible in the bud, but almost obscured when the mass of stamens breaks out.

The rose apple fruit is small and round, marked by the sepals which cling over a depression at its tip. It is creamy and pinkish in color, with a crisp flesh that tastes as roses smell. Although this flavor is delicate, it persists even when the fruit is made into jelly.

40

Sausage Tree

Kigelia pinnata De Condolle
Bignonia family
Tropical West Africa

THE FRUITS of this tree are a horticultural curiosity. Dangling on long stems, they suggest huge rolls of sausage, sometimes two feet long and five inches in diameter. They are covered with a rough, grey skin and are filled with tough fibers in which the seeds are embedded. The flowers also hang on long stems, the buds turning upright in chandelier fashion. A few buds open each night and fall in the morning. The flowers are a dark, velvety, carrion red inside, yellow outside. They have a disagreeable smell which attracts insects. Tubular in form, they open to four lobes, one of which is notched. The flower is about five inches across. The pistil and five yellow stamens rise in the center of the flower. To secure the largest fruits, cross-pollination is necessary. Self-pollinated fruits are short and melon shaped.

The tree is spreading, with very stiff, rough leaves which fall once a year and are replaced in about ten days. The leaves are compound, each leaflet being about five inches long.

White Champak or
Pak-lan

Michelia alba De Condolle
Magnolia family
Java

THE INTENSE fragrance and heavy, ivory-colored, waxen quality of the petals indicate the relationship of this michelia to the magnolias. It was brought to Hawaii by the Chinese and is still seen chiefly in their gardens. Their name for it, *pak-lan*, means white orchid. The pointed buds, about two inches long, grow upright in leaf axils near the ends of the branches. Each is encased in a calyx of the "nightcap" variety, which slips off as the flower opens. The narrow waxen petals are numerous and radiate around the greenish pistil. The flowers are rather inconspicuous, but easily located by their heavy scent.

The tree grows upright and attains about thirty feet. Its pointed, wavy-edged leaves are glossy, leathery, and light green.

The orange champak *(Michelia champaca)* is closely related and similar in appearance, except that the flowers are a creamy orange color.

Kou Haole or Geiger Tree

Cordia sebestena Linnaeus
Heliotrope family
Tropical America

RICH ORANGE red flowers, one to two inches across, appear scatteringly on this small tree for most of the year. They are tubular, spreading into five or seven lobes which are frilled and crepy. Short, light-colored stamens appear in the throat. The flowers grow in clusters of buds, one to four of which open at the same time. They are followed by small fruits which turn white and may be eaten.

Leaves of the tree are stiff, rough, and dark green, from three to eight inches long.

The Hawaiian name of *kou* was originally applied to a closely related species (*Cordia subcordata* Lamarck), which is also found in other parts of Polynesia. Its flowers are quite similar in form to the one above but are a buff or light orange color. The wood of this indigenous kou was used for poi bowls by the early Hawaiians.

Gold Tree or Primavera

Tabebuia donnell-smithii Rose
Bignonia family
Central America

THE GOLD tree when not in bloom is rather nondescript in appearance, its smooth, slender, light grey trunk with branches high in the air seeming ungainly. But when these branches suddenly become a mass of purest shining gold the effect is breath-taking. This effect is intensified by the necessity of always looking upward at the flowers against the blue of the sky. Individual blossoms are tubular, with five large, frilled, crepy lobes. They appear while the tree is leafless in clusters on the branch tips. The time of blooming is very irregular; it can be almost any month in the year, but most often it is in spring. Trees growing near each other, however, may have blooming periods at entirely different seasons.

The tree has two types of foliage. On young specimens five to seven leaflets radiate on long stems from one point. On older trees a compound leaf made up of opposite pairs of leaflets is the rule.

44

Tiger's Claw or Indian Coral Tree

Erythrina variegata var. *orientalis* Merr or *E. indica* Lamarck

Legume family

Tropical Asia

TALL trees, bursting into pointed, red blossoms in midwinter and early spring, are appropriately called tiger's claws or coral trees. The flowers are a deep, rich red, very striking on the bare trees at this season. They grow in long clusters which radiate horizontally on woody stems from the ends of the branches. Individual flowers break out of the split side of a pointed calyx. Fundamentally of the pea type, these flowers have one petal much larger than the others, the general effect being that of a pointed claw or feline toe-nail.

The leaves, which appear soon after the flowers, are made up of three triangular leaflets. The pod is black and contains dark red seeds. The branches are thorny.

A closely related tree, which is native to the Hawaiian islands, is called *wili-wili* by the native people. Botanically it is *Erythrina sandwicensis* Degener or *E. monosperma*. It grows in dry places on the islands where it is conspicuous for its pale red, orange, or yellowish flowers, similar in form to the tiger's claw. The bright red seeds of this *wili-wili* are sometimes made into leis by the Hawaiians.

45

Bottle Brush Tree
Callistemon lanceolatus De Condolle
Myrtle family
Australia

46

DROOPING cylindrical spikes of red flowers suggesting the brushes used to clean bottles and test tubes give its common name to this tree. The inflorescence is made up of loose spikes of red flowers of which the stamens are the most conspicuous part. They appear at the branch ends, but when the flowers fade, the branch continues to grow. Branches and flowers droop and sway pendulously, the effect being much like that of a weeping willow. The fine leaves are greyish green, very long, and narrow. New foliage is pinkish. The tree may become over twenty feet high but is usually less.

Buttercup Tree

Cochlospermum hibiscoides Kunth or
Cochlospermum vitifolium Willdenow
Buttercup tree family
Central America

T HE BRILLIANT yellow flowers of
this small tree resemble a giant
buttercup in general form and
color. They have five deeply
notched petals of rich golden yellow which inclose a mass of gold-
en orange stamens of irregular
length. Each flower is about four
inches across. They begin to appear in October and remain scatteringly on the tree until May. For
a part of this period the tree is
usually leafless, making its color
conspicuous.

The leaves are hand-shaped,
made up of five to seven leaflets.
The central leaflet is long and
pointed, and all are strongly veined. The tree is slender and upright and will attain about twenty
feet in height. The bark is dark
and smooth.

Pink and White Shower Tree

Cassia javanica Linnaeus
Legume family
Java

GREAT feathery masses of unevenly tinted, pink flowers cover this small tree, suggesting in their luxuriance and variable coloring the apple blossoms of the temperate zone. The flowers grow from the main branches on short branchlets, so close together that the branches are often completely enwrapped. The effect has been compared to a huge pink carnation lei. Each flower is made up of five similar petals, from the center of which protrudes a tuft of yellow stamens and a green style. Each petal is palest pink or white, with deeper pink veinings. Eventually, the pink fades, adding to the variegated effect. The calyx and stem are dark red. The trees remain in bloom for months, some opening earlier and some later, but the peak of the season is in June.

The leaves fall off before the blooming period begins, but start to reappear soon after, so that toward the end the flowers make a sharp contrast with the fresh green of the new leaves. Each leaf is of feather form. The leaflets number up to fifteen pairs and are rounded and about an inch long. The tree never becomes large and is often picturesquely irregular in form. Long, cylindrical pods hang on after the leaves and flowers have fallen.

48

Coral Shower Tree
Cassia grandis Linnaeus
Legume family
Tropical America

EARLIEST of the shower trees to bloom in Hawaii is the one which has come to be known as the coral shower or sometimes as the pink shower. (But it is not to be confused with the later-blooming pink and white shower, opposite.) The coral shower blooms during March, April, and May. The flower buds are particularly attractive, being round, velvety balls of delicate, pinkish lavender. The flowers grow on short stalks from the branches and in good specimens they completely cover the branches. The five petals around the stamens are a soft peach pink.

Leaves appear after the first blossoms, the new foliage being pinkish. They are pinnate, with the leaflets rather large. The pods are cylindrical and dark brown. The tree attains greater size, with age, than any of the other shower trees.

50

Golden Shower Tree
Cassia fistula Linnaeus
Legume family
India
(opposite, top)

IMMENSE pendant bunches of large, yellow blossoms, hanging in grapelike clusters among the leaves, explain the popular name of the golden shower tree. The yellow blooms sometimes cover the tree so completely they overwhelm the foliage and make it look as if the tree were standing in sunshine, when around it all is in shadow. The golden yellow flowers, although of basic pea form, have their five petals of almost the same shape and form. They are noticeably veined. From the center project the long, curving pistil and a few stamens. The pistil develops, in the course of a year, into a long, straight, cylindrical, black pod, sometimes three feet in length. In India it has inspired the name of pudding-pipe tree, but this name is not used in Hawaii.

The tree becomes fairly large, with smooth, grey bark. The leaves usually remain throughout the year, but are renewed in the early summer. Each leaf is a foot long with four to eight leaflets about two inches long.

Rainbow Shower Tree
Cassia hybrida
(Cassia javanica × Cassia fistula)
Legume family
Horticultural
(opposite, bottom)

IT WAS probably inevitable that cross-pollination should take place between the golden *Cassia fistula* and the pink and white *Cassia javanica*. The many "rainbow showers" resulting from this cross are among the most beautiful of all Hawaii's flowering trees. For, like so many hybrids, they are often more floriferous and more attractive than either parent. No two of the hybrids are quite alike, although they tend to average a peach or apricot coloring, merging the pink and yellow of the parents. However, some are a pale creamy hue, others the clean sunshine yellow of the golden shower. The colors may deepen into a rich orange pink. At the height of their bloom some trees seem to be almost solid masses of fluffy bloom. Others hold more sparse, open clusters. A tree may sometimes show two colors, usually due to the outside of the bud being orange pink while the inside is yellow. The size and form of the tree and its foliage also vary. The blooming period is generally later than that of either parent and may last well into September.

51

52

Plumeria, Melia, or Frangipani

Plumeria acutifolia Poiret
Periwinkle family
Tropical America

ONE OF the most popular of Hawaiian flower leis is made of the thick, velvety flowers of the plumeria. They are long lasting and have a fine fragrance. The flower is commonly called plumeria in Hawaii, or, as the lei women may say, *pumeli* or *melia*. The name was derived from the French botanist, Plumier, but as a mistake was made in the official spelling, the genus is now properly designated plumeria, not plumiera. In India and Ceylon, where it is extensively grown, it is known by the romantic name of *frangipani*.

The tree has stiff, blunt, forking branches. In spring the flowers appear at the tips of the branches in close, flat, picturesque clusters. The tree continues to bloom after the foliage comes out, until winter. The flowers have five rounded petals, spreading from a short tube. They are a clear yellow with creamy white edges and backs.

The leaves are long and pointed at both ends. The milky juice of this plant is poisonous.

A white species with a yellow center, *P. obtusa,* is called Singapore plumeria although it is also of American origin. It has darker, more oblong leaves, which remain on the tree all year. The flower clusters appear on long stalks. Individual flowers are larger than the common variety and bloom continuously, although they are sparse in winter.

A deep cerise species is *P. rubra.* Flowers are smaller and the petals more pointed than on the common yellow and white. The clusters appear on long, thick stalks. Hybrids of this and the common plumeria have produced innumerable variations in pink and red, some more attractive than others. One especially beautiful hybrid is deep orange pink, named after Gerrit Wilder, its originator.

Octopus or Umbrella Tree

Brassaia actinophylla Endlicher
Panax family
Australia
(no illustration)

Australian plants are sometimes as peculiar as Australian animals. The long radiating arms of this tree's inflorescence invariably attract attention because they suggest an octopus. Each arm may be three feet or more long. The likeness to octopus tentacles is heightened by the row of the small, dark red flower heads along the arm, which suggest the creature's suckers. The flowers are fleshy and indistinct in form. They are followed by small, dark purple fruits.

Almost equally curious are the leaves. They are radially divided at the end of a long leafstalk, suggesting the name, umbrella tree. The leaflets may be twelve inches long and are broad and leathery. The tree is of upright, slender form with few branches.

Chapter Three

Flowering Vines

VINES, which sprawl over rocks and banks or climb high on walls or trees to hang out floral tapestries and banners, make up one of the most colorful and interesting chapters on Hawaiian flowers. While some are everblooming, most have a season when they suddenly put on a brilliant display of color, that often becomes one of the conspicuous sights of the islands. Vines are rather easy to identify, due to their habit of growth and the fact that few resemble each other enough to be confusing.

Laurel-Leaved Thunbergia

Thunbergia laurifolia Lindley
Acanthus family
India

A VINE carrying clusters of large, lavender blue flowers is sometimes called purple allamanda in Hawaii, although it is not related to the allamandas at all. On the contrary, its flower resembles those of its cousin, the large-flowered thunbergia, although the foliage of the two vines is quite different. The leaves are laurel-like, narrow, pointed, smooth, and leathery. The individual flowers are rounder, flatter, and smoother than the other, and the clusters of buds and flowers are shorter. The color approaches a clear purplish blue, but the throat of the tube is yellow. Altogether it forms one of the finest blue flowers in the tropics and has been called one of the most beautiful blue vines in the world.

Thunbergia

Thunbergia fragrans Roxburgh
Acanthus family
India

A SMALL creeping and climbing vine with delicate, white, tubular flowers is also one of the thunbergias. The flowers appear singly along the stem. They have five lobes and are scentless, in spite of the name *"fragrans."* The twining stems are square. The leaves are opposite, pointed, and lobed.

Another small creeping thunbergia has cream- or buff-colored flowers with a deep maroon or purple throat. Called sometimes "black-eyed susan" it is *Thunbergia alata* Bojer.

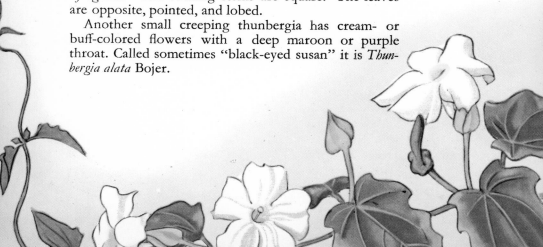

Large-Flowered Thunbergia
Thunbergia grandiflora Roxburgh
Acanthus family
India

IN HONOLULU the white variety of this large-flowered thunbergia is more often seen than the blue. One of the most dramatic and conspicuous of vines, it drops long strings of large, white flowers against its leafy background or forms a swaying canopy when grown along wires or the rafters of an arbor. These strings of flowers and buds may be two or three feet long. Individual flowers, which average about three inches across, have five lobes opening from a short tube with a greenish throat. They bloom all the year, but are at their best in the spring.

The large leaves of this vine are irregular in shape, being often in the form of an angular heart, or they may be lobed or oval. They are rough to the touch.

While the white variety is much more commonly seen in Honolulu, the type flower is a delicate lavender blue. It is sometimes called blue sky flower or Bengal trumpet.

57

Scented Star Jasmine

Jasminum pubescens Willde
Olive family
India

IN MANY places outside Hawaii the term "star jasmine" is applied to a woody vine with small, white, pinwheel-shaped flowers. This is not a true jasmine but botanically it is *Trachelospermum jasminoides*. Hawaii uses the words "star jasmine" to designate several true jasmines which look very much alike. The one most often seen→

Pikake

Jasminum sambac Solander
Olive family
India

THIS favorite lei flower is also a true jasmine, a native of India where it is very popular. Both plant and flower are much like the one above. It is generally grown commercially to produce flowers for leis, but is not often seen in gardens. This is the flower which the Chinese use to scent their jasmine tea.

➡ (usually as a ground cover), is scentless, with flowers like thin, white stars with four to nine points radiating from a slender tube. The flowers emerge from a hairy calyx, its lobes so slender as to be almost threadlike. Leaves are opposite and slightly rough or downy.

The plant which is called "scented star jasmine" appears to be a variety of the one above with the same hairy calyx and leaves. The flowers, however, have a delicate scent, suggesting lilacs. They are larger, thicker, more waxen, and usually have six lobes.

Jade Vine

Strongylodon macrobotrys A. Grey
Legume, pea subfamily
Philippines

Flowers of a bright, bluish jade-green hang on this vine in long spectacular clusters. The hue is probably the rarest in the whole world of flowers. Most people, seeing it for the first time, can hardly believe the color is natural. Hanging among the green leaves it is not so spectacular as when viewed against a dark background. Belonging to the pea group, the flowers are basically of this pattern, but the keels are very long and pointed, the wings bent to a picturesque outline. Individual flowers are about two inches long, with a thick, soft texture. They are successful for leis and are long lasting. The blossoms hang in small groups by blue stems from the main flowering stalk. This may reach four and a half feet in length in good specimens.

The vine is a rampant twiner which climbs high into the trees in its native rain forests on Luzon. Leaves are three-parted, each leaflet small and regular. New foliage is brownish and hangs limp.

Chinese Star Jasmine

Trachelospermum jasminoides
(Lindl.) Lemaire
Periwinkle family
South China

AMONG the most fragrant of flowers are the little, white pinwheels appearing on this vine. They are delicate, starry blossoms, but at the height of bloom in the spring they may make the vine almost completely white and fill the air around with intoxicating scent.

The plant is a shrubby, woody vine. Its leaves are smooth, dark green, waxy, and of medium size. It is not a jasmine, although it is usually thought to be, and the resemblance is noted in its specific name. In some localities, but not in Hawaii, it is called simply star jasmine. Here that name is reserved for the *Jasminum pubescens*.

61

Purple Bignonia

Bignonia magnifica Bull
Bignonia family
Colombia

A VINE with close, green foliage often attracts attention because of its tubular, purplish flowers. They are about two inches long and appear most of the year. The tube is whitish toward the base and broadens into five lobes. Two smooth, leathery leaflets about four inches long make up the leaf. The vine climbs by tendrils.

Cup of Gold

Solandra guttata Don
Tomato family
Mexico

A MAGNIFICENT flower is the great cup of gold blossom. It could be more appropriately called a golden chalice, since the blossom is nine inches long and wide in proportion. It is the rich golden color of a ripe banana, and the brownish streaks on the petals increase this suggestion. Its fragrance, however, is the enchanting scent of ripe apricots. When once the heavy, waxen buds begin to unfold, the petals move so rapidly that their movements can be seen. Blooms appear in January and continue for two or three months.

The leaves are large, thick, and rather pointed. The vine is woody, high climbing, and large.

The silver cup *Solandra grandi-flora* Swartz, is a flower of similar size and general appearance but its color is creamy white.

63

Bleeding Heart or Bag Flower

Clerodendron thomsonae Balfour
Verbena family
West Africa

THE QUAINT, little red and white flowers of this small, sprawling vine appear in open clusters during the winter and spring months. The crimson portion is the true flower, while the "heart" or "bag" is the white calyx. The red flower is composed of a slender tube extending beyond the calyx and spreading into five lobes. A group of fine stamens protrudes beyond the flower. The leaves are opposite, large, dark green, and slightly rough to the touch.

Cat's Claw Climber

Doxanthus unguis-cati Rehder or
Bignonia unguis-cati Linnaeus
Bignonia family
Tropical America

WHEN THE cat's claw climber blooms in spring, a cloth of pure gold is flung over walls and trees. The individual flowers are of purest canary yellow and are shaped like small trumpets opening to five lobes. Each is about two inches long. They grow in clusters of three or more. The ground is often carpeted with yellow when they fall.

The vine's branches are rather slender. They cling to walls or tree trunks with tiny, three-pronged tendrils much like a cat's claw, hence the common name. It is also called hug-me-tight. The leaves are made up of two leaflets, between which grows the three-pronged tendril. The leaflets are about three inches long, pointed, and with wavy edges.

65

Garlic-Scented Vine

Cydista aequinoctialis Miers
Bignonia family
Tropical America

A VINE with attractive clusters of orchid-colored, gloxinia-like flowers radiates a most disagreeable odor of garlic and so inevitably is known as garlic vine. Since it has periods of special bloom in spring and fall, it is also called the equinox vine, but in Hawaii its flowers are usually to be found all the year round. The white throated tube of the blossom is slightly flattened, then broadens into five lobes of purplish-orchid color. The color becomes lighter as the flower fades. At the bottom of the tube are yellow stamens. The flowers appear in clusters usually of six to ten.

The leaves are rich glossy green, growing in opposite pairs in such a way that four of them seem to be emerging from one point on the stem. A straight tendril sometimes extends from between the pairs near the end of the branch.

Wax Vine

Hoya carnosa R. Brown
Milkweed family
South China

FRAGRANT, waxy, white flowers grow in clusters, their stems radiating from a single point on the main stem. The small blossoms are shaped like creamy white stars, and each flower contains a smaller white star in its center, against a pink flush. In another variety, the flower is brownish. Hoya blossoms give off a strong fragrance, especially in the evening.

The vine is a twiner, with roots appearing along the stems. The leaves are thick, shining, oval, and usually overshadow the flowers.

67

Orchid Vine or Brazilian Golden Vine

Stigmatophyllum ciliatum A. Jussieu
and *Stigmatophyllum littorale* A.
Jussieu
Malpighia family
Tropical America

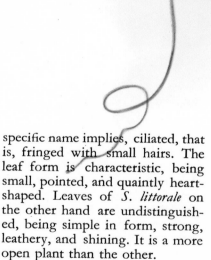

TWO UNUSUALLY beautiful vines,
seen rarely as yet in Honolulu
gardens, are both called orchid
vine, probably from the resemblance of their small, yellow flowers
to little yellow orchids. They are
in no way related to the orchids,
but the two are closely related to
each other. They resemble each
other so much, in fact, that it
might be difficult to distinguish
them readily were it not for their
leaves. These have characteristics
which are easily noticed.

Leaves of *Stigmatophyllum ciliatum*
(upper illustration) are, as their
specific name implies, ciliated, that
is, fringed with small hairs. The
leaf form is characteristic, being
small, pointed, and quaintly heart-
shaped. Leaves of *S. littorale* on
the other hand are undistinguished, being simple in form, strong,
leathery, and shining. It is a more
open plant than the other.

The flowers of both are of the
clearest canary yellow, similar in
form, and having five unequal
petals of crepy, satiny texture. *S.
ciliatum* is everblooming. Its flowers are larger individually, but the
clusters are smaller. *S. littorale*
blooms in the late winter and is
marked by its immense, loose
clusters of tiny flowers.

68

Phanera

Bauhinia corymbosa Roxburgh
Legume, senna subfamily
South China

THIS IS a woody vine or sprawling shrub that branches from the ground and climbs by tendrils. During the summer months it carries large, loose clusters of small, pinkish flowers. Each is about an inch across with five frilled petals. They are white or flushed with pink. Several long, bright red stamens projecting from the center increase the pinkish effect. The flowers are followed by brown pods.

The leaves are small, one or two inches long, and deeply cleft into two rounded sections.

Gloriosa Lily or
Climbing Lily

Gloriosa rothschildiana O'Brien
Lily family
Tropical Africa

THIS VINE attracts attention at once by the curious way in which the tip of each broad, pointed leaf is elongated in to a ten- dril. The plant can climb by these to ten feet or more. The bright red and yellow flowers are unusual also, the six petals being long and narrow, with crisp, rippled edges. They curve upward in a cluster, and the six stamens project conspicuously. As the flower fades the bright red becomes purplish.

Beaumontia

Beaumontia jerdoniana Wight
Periwinkle family
India

THE LARGE, papery white flower cups, with a touch of palest green in the center, give an almost ethereal quality to the beaumontia. The flowers have a delicate, faint fragrance which matches their fragile beauty. Individuals are bell-shaped, with five lobes, about six inches across. From the center rise five white stamens joined at their tips. The backs of the petals are slightly stained with brown, and the small calyxes are brown also. The flowers grow in large clusters of buds, of which five or six at a time may open. The blooming season is winter and spring. They are popular for wedding bouquets.

The woody vine is a rampant grower with large, smooth leaves, prominently veined.

71

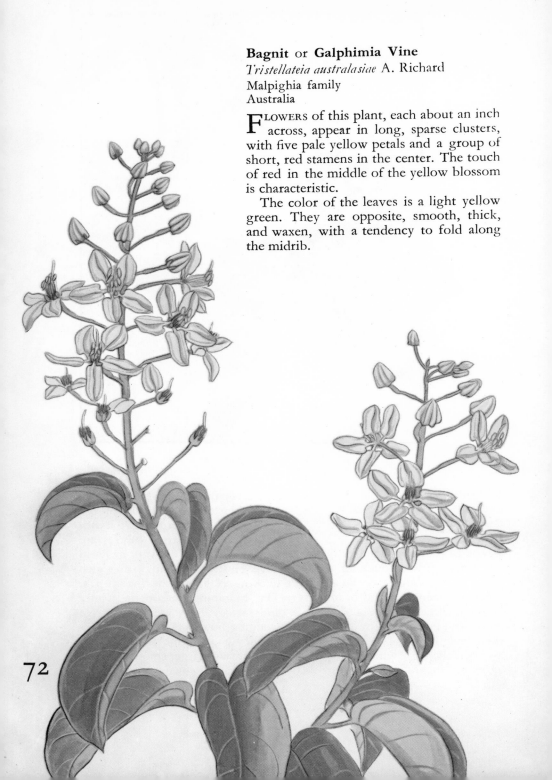

Bagnit or Galphimia Vine

Tristellateia australasiae A. Richard
Malpighia family
Australia

FLOWERS of this plant, each about an inch across, appear in long, sparse clusters, with five pale yellow petals and a group of short, red stamens in the center. The touch of red in the middle of the yellow blossom is characteristic.

The color of the leaves is a light yellow green. They are opposite, smooth, thick, and waxen, with a tendency to fold along the midrib.

72

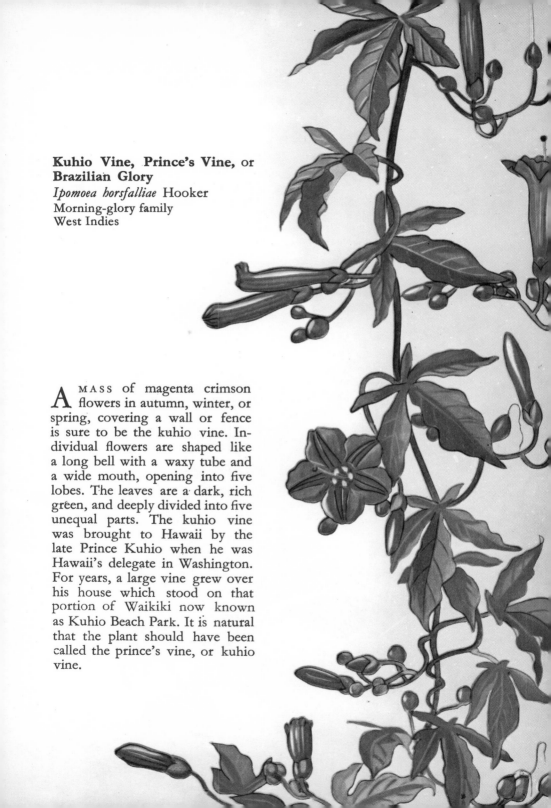

Kuhio Vine, Prince's Vine, or Brazilian Glory

Ipomoea horsfalliae Hooker
Morning-glory family
West Indies

A MASS of magenta crimson flowers in autumn, winter, or spring, covering a wall or fence is sure to be the kuhio vine. Individual flowers are shaped like a long bell with a waxy tube and a wide mouth, opening into five lobes. The leaves are a dark, rich green, and deeply divided into five unequal parts. The kuhio vine was brought to Hawaii by the late Prince Kuhio when he was Hawaii's delegate in Washington. For years, a large vine grew over his house which stood on that portion of Waikiki now known as Kuhio Beach Park. It is natural that the plant should have been called the prince's vine, or kuhio vine.

Stephanotis
Stephanotis floribunda Brongniart
Milkweed family
Madagascar

STEPHANOTIS flowers are white, waxy trumpets with a penetrating fragrance which suggests hyacinths. Each flower is about two inches long, with five lobes spreading at the end of the tube. They hang in clusters of six or eight. The flowers last very well when cut and are often made into leis. The blooming season is April to October.

The leaves are thick, glossy, and dark green. They may have an indentation at the tip. The woody vine is rather sparse, depending on the attractiveness of the leaves and the flowers for its appeal.

Pandorea

Pandorea brycei (N.E. Brown)
  Rehder
Bignonia family
Rhodesia

A VINE with attractive pink flowers streaked with red is sometimes seen on fences. The tubular flowers open to five crepy lobes. The leaves are compound, with delicate, pointed leaflets, usually seven to eleven per leaf. The vine is woody and rather open but it grows vigorously.

Another vine very similar to this one is the bower plant from Australia *(Pandorea jasminoides)* which has pale pink or white flowers or white with a pink throat.

75

Butterfly Pea

Clitoria ternatea Linnaeus
Legume family
Origin uncertain

Blossoms of a true cerulean blue are exceedingly rare in the flower world, but those of the butterfly pea are of this hue. Though small and scattered on the vine, these little flowers are delightful for their gorgeous color and unusual shape. As members of the pea family, they have the "banner," or large top petal, while the "wings" are very small. The banner usually has a white mark at the base. Sometimes the flowers occur double, and there is also a white variety.

The foliage is compound, the leaflets being rounded. The plant, which is an annual in colder climates, grows rather thickly. The dried pealike pods which follow the flowers hang on the vine a long time. The seeds grow easily.

The plant gets its name from the island of Ternate in the East Indies, but is considered a cosmopolitan in the tropics.

Orange Trumpet or Huapala

Pyrostegia ignea (Vell.) Presl or
Bignonia venusta Ker
Bignonia family
Brazil

ONE OF the spectacular events in Hawaii's floral calendar is the blooming of the huapala. Beginning in January, walls of green may turn into a sheet of flaming orange, the masses of flowers seeming like small tongues of fire running over the entire vine.

Blossoms grow in end racemes, each individual flower a long, slender tube, its tip curving back into four or five lobes. These often form the even outline of a cross, with the fourth lobe curiously split to make the five-part flower. The style and four stamens extend beyond the tube. When the flower begins to fade, the tube slips loose, but is often caught by the enlarged tip of the style, so that it still hangs awhile on the vine to add its color to the mass.

The leaves are glossy and bright green, often growing as three rather pointed leaflets.

Porana Vine or Snow Creeper
Porana paniculata Roxburgh
Morning-glory family
India and Malaya

A MASS of tiny, white flowers, so small and so numerous they suggest a drift of smoke or a light fall of snow, is the porana vine in bloom. The flowering period is autumn and winter. The rest of the year the plant carries its large, greyish green, feltlike leaves in thick profusion. The leaves are opposite, either heart-shaped or oval.

Individual flowers are shaped like minute, white morning-glories, the porana being a member of this family. The tiny, white blossoms appear in huge lacy panicles at the ends of the branches.

In its native habitat of India and Malaya, the vines grow to a great height in the jungles. Its name is said to be derived from the Javanese name.

78

Mauna Loa Vine

Canavalia microcarpa De Candolle
Legume, pea subfamily
Mascarene Islands

THE CHIEF interest in this small, annual pea vine is the use of its flowers to make the old-fashioned mauna loa leis, named after the mountain on the Big Island of Hawaii. The vine is often seen growing in waste places with its reddish stems and three triangular leaflets. The small, pink or lavender, pea-shaped flowers appear in sparse clusters on long stems. They are followed by broad pods filled with dark, rounded seeds.

The sculptured effect of a mauna loa lei is obtained by stringing the flowers crosswise through the calyx. The string is hen laid on a flat surface and the individual flowers turned alternately right and left. A narrow strip of adhesive tape is placed along the center length of the lei and held in place with pins. The large top petal of each flower is then turned back and stuck down, alternately, left and right. The keels of the flowers form the bordering projections.

Petrea or Sandpaper Vine

Petrea volubilis Linnaeus
Verbena family
Tropical America

AN EXCITING experience in Hawaii is to come upon the petrea in full bloom. Cascading racemes of lavender blue flowers cover the plant completely, turning it into a tumbling fall of lacy blue. What seems at first to be the flower is really the calyx, which is five-pointed, starlike, and periwinkle blue. The true flower is a rich violet in color and looks something like a true violet flower growing in the center of the calyx star. This true blossom falls off the plant in a day or two but the calyx remains. Each raceme is seven or eight inches long and carries fifteen to thirty flowers. The plant blooms several times during the year, but is at its best in spring.

The vines are woody and high climbing. The leaves are very rough to the touch, giving the plant its popular name.

Mexican Creeper

Antigonon leptopus Hooker and
  Arnott
Buckwheat family
Mexico

L ACY MASSES of small, bright
   pink or cerise flowers, clam-
bering by curling tendrils over
trees, rocks, or weeds, proclaim the
Mexican creeper. In its native
Mexico it is called chain of love,
that is, *cadena de amor,* since the
flowers suggest a string of small,
pink hearts. The Mexicans also
give it other sentimental names
such as *rosa de montana* and *corallita.*

The flower stems branch in a
rather angular and picturesque
way. The leaves are heart-shaped,
rough, and have wavy margins.
The colored portion of the flower
is the calyx as there are no petals.
After the seeds dry, they often
hang on the plant a long time.

There is a white variety that is
smaller and very dainty.

Wood Rose, Ceylon Morning-glory, or **Spanish Arbor Vine**

Ipomoea tuberosa Linnaeus
Morning-glory family
Origin uncertain

ONE OF the most attractive of plant novelties is the wood rose which looks indeed like some wonderful bit of carving, rubbed to an exquisite satiny brown finish. The "rose," however, is really the dried seed pod of a species of morning-glory, as anyone familiar with the ordinary morning-glory seed will at once notice. The central ball holds the seeds, while the dried, enlarged calyx which surrounds it appears as the "petals" of the wood rose.

In Hawaii, the vine is a perennial, grown from seeds. Its strong shoots spread rampantly during the summer months, climbing high into trees or covering buildings and fences. The leaf is divided into seven pointed lobes. The flowers first appear in autumn. They are small, yellow, rather inconspicuous, and shaped like the small, yellow morning-glory which they really are. After they drop, the calyx begins to develop until it becomes like an immense, pointed, cream-colored bud. As this begins to dry, it opens and in a few days, the "wood rose" is stiff and brown. About three months are required from the time the blossom appears until the seed pod is ready to cut. These pods may be used as long-lived decorations. And since the flowers appear at intervals along the stem, graceful lengths with many pods can be obtained for flower arrangements. Beetles and other insects often damage these pods.

83

Bougainvilleas

Bougainvillea spectabilis Willdenow
Four o'clock family
Brazil

MASSES of purple bougainvillea are a familiar sight in sub-tropical countries. But other colors, such as crimson, orange, white, and pink are seen in Hawaii. Botanically there are two purple forms. *B. spectabilis* is seen as masses of color in the spring. Its variety *parviflora,* is everblooming, but more sparse.

The rich crimson lake bougainvillea *(B. glabra* var. *sanderiana)* seems to be the most popular in Honolulu, perhaps because it hangs out its long sprays in winter and early spring when other flowers are not plentiful. A variety sometimes has bright orange flowers and occasionally on the same plant may be seen the crimson red also. Such a plant is known as rainbow bougainvillea.

The red brick or tawny orange bougainvillea is *B. spectabilis* var. *lateritia*. Its blooming period is seasonal, the flowers usually appearing only in winter and spring.

A white form, probably *B. glabra* var. *sanderiana,* is occasionally seen. With its periodic masses of greenish white flowers it makes a striking effect. Seen also are one or more pale-pink- or orchid-colored forms whose botanical affinities are uncertain. The unusual colors are horticultural variants.

The color of bougainvillea flowers is due, not to the actual flowers but to the colored leaves which form a three-part bract around the true flower. The latter is small, yellow, tubular, and might be mistaken for the ordinary yellow center of the flower. The plant was named after Louis de Bougainville, a French navigator of the eighteenth century, who found it in Rio de Janeiro.

85

Yellow Allamanda

Allamanda cathartica var. *hendersonii* (Bull) Raffill
Periwinkle family
Brazil

Large, velvety, bright yellow flowers, growing on a sprawling vine or shrub are allamandas. The big, yellow flowers have a tube which spreads into five large, thick lobes. They grow in terminal clusters, two or three buds opening at a time. The buds are pointed, brownish in color, and look as if they had been varnished. The brown color blotches the back of the petals and streaks the throat of the tube. Leaves are thick, smooth, pointed, and usually a light green. They tend to appear in fours, forming a cross or whorl where they join the stem.

The original species, differing from the large variety above, is smaller, doesn't have brown on the buds, and its leaves are hairy beneath.

86

Chapter Four

Tropical Shrubs

IN HAWAII the woody shrubs make up the bulk of the garden material generally seen. They form a convenient and permanent component for an all-year garden because, once established, they continue to grow and bloom indefinitely. Their limited size also makes them useful for many purposes in the average garden. They meet the needs of the all-year-garden owner in another way also. Where every day is a gardening day, the average person cannot maintain that high enthusiasm for planting and digging which marks spring in temperate areas. The average tropical gardener finds it easier to fill his beds with something that demands but little attention and spend his more tempered enthusiasm on some floral hobby.

HIBISCUS

OUTSTANDING among Hawaii's shrubs is, of course, the hibiscus. This group, producing large and beautiful flowers, is so easily grown

garden holds one or many plants. The flowers generally cross-pollinate and seed easily, and the new hybrids may possess spectacular new forms and color combinations. So many people have experimented with cross-breeding that today Hawaii has the largest number of hybrids known anywhere. It is estimated there are some five thousand.

The hibiscus flower possesses the unusual trait of not wilting for a day after it is picked. Since it lasts only one day anyway and for that day will stay as fresh, without water, as if left on the bush, the flowers can be used for many forms of floral decoration. For leis, however, the hibiscus blossom is not successful because it is easily crushed and bruised and the coloring may stain clothing.

It is interesting that Hawaii has a number of native hibiscus generally called koki'o. They occur in several colors varying from island to island and from area to area. Scientists are often uncertain whether certain ones are species or varieties. But from the gardener's point of view the native hibiscus cannot be of much interest. In general the plants will not grow away from their native districts, and for the most part their flowers are rather small and uninteresting. An exception to this is the Oahu white.

1. Koki'o or Native Hawaiian White Hibiscus
Hibiscus arnottianus Gray

AMONG the most ornamental of Hawaii's native species of hibiscus is this white one, usually with a red staminal column. It grows as a tall shrub or as a small tree with smooth, grey bark. The five flower petals are several inches long, the leaves somewhat varied, but usually oval, some-

times with scalloped edges. The outstanding characteristic of this species is its fragrance, a rare thing among hibiscus. This characteristic has been transmitted to some of its many hybrid descendants. Growing wild between one thousand and three thousand feet above sea level, the plant is found in some island gardens.

2. Common Red or Chinese Hibiscus

Hibiscus rosa-sinensis Linnaeus
South China

FIVE RED petals forming a bell, about five inches across, from which rises a long staminal column, mark the little China hibiscus, a typical example of the genera. The column is covered with stamens and at its tip it branches into a five-parted, crystalline, red style. The plant may sometimes attain twenty feet but is usually much less. Its leaves are coarsely toothed and roughly oval or elongated in form. There are double varieties, and the red coloring varies from orange red to flag red.

This plant has entered into many hybrids. In fact the average red hibiscus seen in Hawaii today is more apt to be a hybrid than the species.

3. Coral Hibiscus

Hibiscus schizopetalus (Mast)
Hooker
East Africa

A SMALL reddish hibiscus which differs markedly from the average is this one, conspicuous for its drooping, swaying grace and lacy form. The flower stem is long and thin, so the head falls forward. Its five petals are deeply fringed and curl back against the stem. They are red, with white and yellow margins. Hanging far down below the flower is the long

staminal column, which sways in the least breeze. The plant also has long, thin branches, and very fine foliage.

This species, with its special characteristics, has entered into many crosses, adding grace and often a frilled edge to the petals. In fact it is safe to assume that any Hawaiian hybrid which has a tendency to droop or has an extra long column has this plant among its ancestors.

4. Waterfall or Butterfly Hybrid Hibiscus

OFTEN seen in Hawaiian gardens is a pink hibiscus plant which is tall, slender, drooping, and almost always covered with many flowers. Being tall and floriferous, it is very useful as garden material, although individual flowers are usually rather undistinguished. This plant is believed to be a hybrid of the native white and the coral species. Its height and general blossom form are from the native white, while its drooping, graceful, and long staminal column is from the coral parent.

5. Yellow Hybrid Hibiscus

THERE are many species of hibiscus around the world and some of these have been introduced informally into Hawaii with no records kept. Among these, apparently, were yellows which probably were hybrids when brought in. They have entered other crosses, so that Hawaii possesses today a large assortment of highly ornamental yellow-flowering hibiscus. Some are double and many are large. Colors range from pale lemon to deep orange yellow, true orange, and orange red, with combinations of these and other colors. As these plants were once rare and highly valued they have been better preserved than many others.

Red Justicia or Odontonema

Justicia coccinea or
Odontonema strictum Kuntze
Acanthus family
Tropical America

THIS PLANT bears 'stiff, upright spikes of red flowers, each a waxy little cornucopia with five small lobes. It rises from a short, red bract. The flower stalk is a mass of buds of which only a few, irregularly up and down its length, develop at a time. This gives it a rather ragged and irregular appearance, but prolongs its blooming season through summer and autumn. The open flowers fall quickly, making it untidy as a cut flower.

The plant is herbaceous, growing from six to eight feet tall in semishade. Its large, pointed leaves are opposite, prominently veined, and a bright glossy green.

Natal Plum

Carissa grandiflora De Candolle
Periwinkle family
South Africa

THE NATAL plum is characterized by its long, sharp thorns, its fragrant, starlike, white flowers, and its bright red fruits, which shine conspicuously among the leaves. Long, needle-like thorns fork out in vicious pairs where the branches divide. They make the plant practically impenetrable, and for this reason it is sometimes used for hedges.

The small, tubular, white flowers are extremely fragrant and have five waxy petals. The fruits, when ripe, are a bright pinkish red about two inches long. They make an excellent jelly. The leaves are dense, small, thick, leathery, and bluntly pointed. They were evidently designed to withstand dryness, and the plant will grow under very dry conditions. It will attain the size of a small tree or can be kept trimmed into a shrub or even a formal hedge.

Lady of the Night

Brunfelsia americana Linnaeus
Tomato family
West Indies
(bottom, left)

A BRUNFELSIA with creamy white flowers is known by the romantic name of "lady of the night," from its habit of turning fragrant after dark. The flowers, which appear in spring, differ from the blue brunfelsia in length of tube as well as color, the tube being longer. The foliage is often yellow green. The shrub is larger than the blue-flowering species and grows more quickly.

Brunfelsia or Yesterday-Today-and-Tomorrow

Brunfelsia latifolia (Hook) Benthan
Tomato family
Brazil
(bottom, right)

A SHRUB, beautifully covered at intervals during the spring and autumn with flowers of three colors, blue, lavender, and white, is called yesterday-today-and-tomorrow because of this peculiarity. The various colorings are due to the fading of the flowers. They are a rich lavender blue when they first open, then change to pale lavender, and finally to almost white before they fall. The brightly colored ones show a white eye in the center where the white tube makes a tiny ring in the blue. The tube opens into five lobes which superficially suggest a pansy. They have a delicate, pungent scent.

The plant is woody, with light grey bark and dark green leaves. Sometimes the leaves are pointed, or they may be quite blunt. The shrub is slow growing but it may attain eight feet.

THE BLOSSOMS of this shrub resemble, to some extent, the tufted red stamens of the native tree called ohia lehua *(Metrosideros polymorpha)* and so they have been given the common name of "foreign lehua," that is, lehua haole. The shrub is more often seen in gardens than the native species because it thrives at lower levels.

The fluffy, red pompons of the lehua haole are one of the most effective of the island lei flowers. Each is a large, round head of pinkish red stamens, fragile in appearance, but of surprising strength and endurance for lei making. Strung together they create a rope of color that is like feathers. These leis are sold during the winter months.

Although it is slow growing, the plant will attain twelve feet in height. Its leaves are curiously divided into pairs, each of which is further compounded into small leaflets. These are graduated in size, the ones at the end being largest. They are velvety and have two strong, lateral midveins.

Lehua Haole
Calliandra inaequilatera Rusby
Legume, mimosa subfamily
Bolivia

93

Pink Honeysuckle

Lonicera heckrottii Rehder
Honeysuckle family
Origin unknown

THIS HONEYSUCKLE immediately attracts attention because of its color and size. The flowers are of typical form but a bright pink outside, yellow within. They are about two inches long. Buds grow in clusters at the branch tips and open a few at a time. The plant is a straggling shrub, almost a vine. Its leaves are stemless, smooth, oval The two just below the flower are joined in an oblong shape. The plant's origin is unknown but it may be a hybrid.

Oleander

Nerium oleander Linnaeus
Periwinkle family
Asia Minor

OLEANDERS are tall shrubs with numerous grey-barked stems emerging from the ground. Some may reach a height of twenty feet, but the average is nearer eight or ten feet. Their leaves, in groups of three, are slender, pointed, and usually a rather dull green, which makes the plants appear greyish. The branches are tipped with clusters of flowers, some single with five petals, others double. Colors range from white through cream, pink, rose, and red in various tones. This species is scentless, but there is a fragrant species, *Nerium indicum* Miller, which is native to India. The color range is about the same in this group. Flowers are followed by slender seed pods.

All oleanders are poisonous in all their parts.

95

Croton

Codiaeum variegatum (L) Blume
var. *pictum*

Splurge family
Pacific islands

SHRUBS with permanently colored leaves in red, pink, orange, yellow, gold, and bronze, along with green are one of the novelties of the tropics. A number of plants have such colored foliage, but the largest group to possess it is the croton. The native plant, found in Fiji and other Pacific islands is green. The colorful varieties have been developed by horticulturists. There is an almost unlimited number of these variations, and differences extend to the leaf form as well as to coloring. Some leaves are long and narrow, others broad, some are wavy or even twisted, others flat. The color appears in splotches, dots, and lines.

The flowers are inconspicuous, with the sexes separate. Both grow on thin spikes, the male as tiny heads of white stamens, the female developing into small, green fruits.

Bush Thunbergia

Thunbergia erecta T. Anderson
Acanthus family
Tropical West Africa

RICH PURPLE blue flowers with golden throats make this blossoming shrub particularly attractive. The flower is made up of a whitish tube emerging from a pair bracts and spreading into five purple lobes. They are thin and velvety in texture. The flower is about two inches long and the same in width. It grows singly in leaf axils and fades almost at once after being picked. There is also a pure-white form with a yellow throat.

The plant is an open, rather straggling shrub which may become five feet high. Its slender branches bear small, opposite leaves, pointed at either end.

97

Crown Flower or
Giant Indian Milkweed
Calotropis gigantea (Linnaeus) Aiton
Milkweed family
India

THE CROWN flower derived its name in Hawaii from the miniature "crowns" which form the center of the flowers. These were popular with Queen Liliuo- kalani, who enjoyed them, pre- sumably, as an emblem of royalty. There are both white- and greyish- lavender-colored varieties. The flowers have five thick, starlike, twisted petals. Above them rises the tiny "crown," holding the stamens and a five-pointed style. Leis can be made from the entire flower, or the crowns can be se- parated and strung, the white ones looking like .carved jade. They have, indeed, been imitated very successfully in carved ivory.

The shrub has thick, light green leaves, which are woolly beneath, and downy stems, with the milky juice of the milkweeds. It will grow to twelve or fifteen feet in upright form, carrying its clusters of flowers at the branch tips. Seed pods seldom mature in Hawaii but when they do they hold a large amount of floss.

Ixora

Ixora macrothyrsa Teysmann and
  Binnendijk
Coffee family
East Indies

LARGE, round "snowball" heads
  of scarlet bloom make the ixora
a very conspicuous shrub. The
small individual flowers have four
lobes spreading from the end of a
long, slender, two inch tube, which
looks, at first glance, like a stem.
The plant can become almost a
small tree, but is usually shrublike.
Its leaves are about a foot long,
narrow, and glossy like those of
the coffee plant to which it is related. Round leis are sometimes
made by stringing the flowers a-
cross the center of the tube.

There are several other species
of ixora growing in Hawaii. Among
them is a white one from Madagascar *(I. odorata)*, which is fragrant.

99

Copper Leaf or Beefsteak Plant

Acalypha wilkesiana J. Mueller-Aargau

Euphorbia family

Fiji

A PLANT with bright red foliage, which might easily be taken for one of the crotons, is really an Acalypha, a relative of the striking chenille plant. Its leaves are large and tend to be triangular in form with slightly scalloped margins. They are basically a bronzy green with wide-spreading blotches of bright red, pink, and brown, giving a total effect of warm red. Insects are attracted to these leaves so they are often full of holes or reduced to lacy outlines.

The small, inconspicuous flowers are of two kinds; pistillate, or female flowers, which appear in small upright spikes with reddish tufts, and staminate, or male, pollen-bearing blossoms, which are brownish and drooping and suggest little rat tails.

The shrub may grow to ten feet. It is often used for hedges, which always stand out brilliantly.

Galphimia or
Rain of Gold
Galphimia glauca Cavanilles or
Thryallis glauca Kuntze
Malpighia family
Southern Mexico

THE NAME "rain of gold" *(lluvia de oro)* by which this plant is known in its native Mexico is very descriptive. A small shrub, with small, glossy, opposite leaves on many fine branches, it carries terminal clusters of tiny, bright golden flowers. The plant is usually covered with these small flower heads, giving a very gay and sunny effect. The flowers are starlike, with five petals. The young branch-tips are reddish. The word "galphimia" is an anagram of the word "malpighia," the name of the family.

Fragrant Clerodendron

Clerodendron fragrans R. Brown var.
pleniflorum Schauer
Verbena family
China

FLAT, TIGHT clusters of small, pinkish flowers, each one like a tiny rosebud, appear over this large shrub in spring. A large, five-pointed, rosy purple calyx surrounds each flower and, extending beyond it, becomes an important feature. At night the blossom develops a distinctive and rather unpleasant scent. It will grow to ten feet, and has large, downy leaves, about ten inches long.

Red Bauhinia

Bauhinia galpini N. E. Brown
Legume, senna subfamily
Africa

THE RICH orange red flowers of this plant suggest a nasturtium or perhaps a small, red orchid with long stamens. There are five petals of equal size and color, each about one and a half inches long. They appear in summer or fall, in clusters of six to ten, and are followed by pods with dark brown seeds.

The plant is a sprawling woody shrub. Its leaves are rounded but divided into two lobes by a bottom cleft. Insects seem to relish them, as they are often eaten to a lacelike skeleton.

103

Aloe

Aloe ciliaris Haworth
Lily family
South Africa

THIS SUCCULENT plant carries a stalk which holds many small, tubular flowers in soft orange red color. They appear in late spring and sometimes again in autumn. Each little tube flower opens at the tip with tiny, greenish segments and the yellow stamens show briefly. Then it closes again.

The plant is made up of thick, scrambling. stems on which the leaves are spirally arranged, crowding toward the tips. The leaves are thick and triangular, with tiny teeth along the edge and whitish coloring near the base.

104

Shrimp Plant
Beloperone guttata Brandegee
Acanthus family
Mexico

A SERIES of bracts, overlapping with scalelike precision for several inches to form an articulated tube, create a flower head that is highly suggestive of the curved tail of a shrimp. These heart-shaped bracts are terra-cotta red or greenish near the top. From behind them emerge (one or two at a time) the small, white, tubular flowers. They have purplish dots on the larger of the two lobes.

The plant sprawls, with thin, weak stems, making it much used as a ground cover. The pointed leaves are opposite, slightly rough to the touch, and about two inches long.

Lasiandra

Tibouchina semidecandra Cogniaux
Melastoma family
Brazil

FLOWERS of royal purple velvet, a rich and exciting color, make this plant conspicuous whenever in bloom. It is not seen often in the warmer parts of Honolulu because it prefers slightly cooler temperatures, but often on mountain roads, where it has escaped, it makes purple masses of bloom. The flowers have five velvety petals and in the center a group of lighter pinkish stamens, which are peculiarly angled. The buds are a bright pinkish red, due to the velvety color of the calyx.

Leaves are almost as attractive as the flowers, being thickly piled with green hairs which create a silver sheen. They are marked laterally by several conspicuous veins. Old leaves scattered over the plant turn bright scarlet and are as noticeable as the flowers.

Golden Eranthemum

Pseuderanthemum reticulatum
 Radlkofer
Acanthus family
Southern Polynesia

CONSPICUOUS for its sunny yellow leaves and dainty, white and purple flowers is a small shrub, which occasionally may attain six feet. Young leaves are a clear yellow or greenish yellow, this coloring surviving on the older foliage as a fine network of yellow venation. The little flowers grow in small spikes at the ends of the branches. They are tubular, the tubes broadening into four lobes, which are white, spotted with purple dots.

107

Singapore Holly
Malpighia coccigera Linnaeus
Malpighia family
West Indies

A PLANT that is neither a holly nor from Singapore, in spite of its common name in Hawaii, has miniature holly-like leaves. They are crisp, shining, and prickly, and grow in small pairs. The upright, slender branches may sometimes attain six feet but are usually less. The plant occasionally breaks into a bloom of delicate, light pink flowers. They grow on longish stems from the leaf axils. Each flower has five slightly fringed petals around yellow stamens. Occasionally these may develop into small, red fruits.

Crown of Thorns
Euphorbia splendens Bojer
Spurge family
Madagascar

THIS PLANT is proclaimed by quantities of very long, sharp thorns on round succulent stems. The flowers appear at all seasons in small bunches, on longish stems. What appears to be two red petals is really a pair of bracts. The plant may become four feet high. Its thorny branches usually twist somewhat and are often bare of leaves. Leaves appearing on the new growth are roundly oblong, pointed toward the stem end, and bright green.

Trailing Lantana

Lantana sellowiana Link and Otto
Verbena family
South America

THIS TRAILING, woody plant seldom grows more than a foot or two high and is generally used as a ground cover. It is dotted with small clusters of rosy lavender flowers, about an inch across. Each cluster is made up of florets which are tiny tubes with five lobes. The foliage is small, stiff, rough, with prominent veins, and each leaf is minutely scalloped. An annual verbena with some-what similar flowers is also used as a ground cover, but the two can be distinguished since the latter is an herbaceous plant.

The familiar red and yellow *Lantana camara* Linnaeus often grows in Hawaii as a weed beside the roads. It escaped after being introduced as a garden plant. Freed from controlling parasites, it grew so riotously that at one time it threatened island agriculture with its dense thickets. The native parasites were introduced, and the plant has since subsided.

Tiare or Tahitian Gardenia
Gardenia taitensis De Condolle
Coffee family
Tahiti

SINGLE, starry, pinwheel flowers, white and very fragrant, characterize that gardenia which is native to the South Seas. The blossoms are extremely popular with the Polynesian people, who make them into leis and wear them in their hair. The plant, however, apparently could not be carried long distances in the sailing canoes, for it was not known in Hawaii until introduced in comparatively recent years.

Each flower has from five to nine points, spreading from the end of a long, slender tube. The leaves are waxen, a rather light green, and tend to be broader near the tip than at the base. They have prominent venation. The shrub may attain six feet. It grows in warmer areas than does the common gardenia and is often seen in seaside gardens.

Christmas Daisy or Christmas Cosmos
Montanoa hibiscifolia (Benth.)
 Schultz Bipontius
Daisy family, helianthus tribe
Guatemala

To FIND ordinary looking white daisies growing in large clusters on a twenty-foot-tall shrub always seems surprising and arouses curiosity about this plant. Although it attains almost the proportions of a small tree, the stems are pithy and are usually cut back after blooming. The leaves suggest those of the hibiscus, hence its specific name. They are downy and actually of two types, one small, pointed, and narrow, the other more conspicuous, large, broad, and with five pointed lobes. The flowering period is December, hence its common name in Honolulu. The blossoms last only about three weeks, but during that time they are always conspicuous. Individual flowers are typical daisies, with eight ray florets, having a white petal around a center of small, yellow florets.

112

Slipper Flower
Pedilanthus tithymaloides Poiteau
Spurge family
Tropical America

A STOCKY, green, succulent plant with quaint, little, slipper-shaped flowers takes its common name from their form. The plant stems, which sometimes attain six feet, are round, scculent, and some may assume a zigzag formation. Leaves are thick and waxy, either all green or white and green in a variegated form. White lines show along the stalks of this form. At certain seasons, the white and green leaves may become stained with pink. Leaves tend to fall off the older stalks. The flowers are borne on small branchlets angling from the stem. On the green plant they are pinkish, on the variegated form a bright red. Each flower is of pointed triangular shape, with the stamens and pistil protruding. The colored portion is a bract.

Madagascar Periwinkle

Vinca rosea Linnaeus or
Lochnera rosea (L) Reichenbach
Periwinkle family
Tropical America

THIS LOW shrub, or perennial, looks like an annual plant of the tropics. It grows about two feet high on herbaceous stems and has oblong leaves, about three inches long, having bluntly pointed tips.

The small flowers, white or rosy pink, have five lobes from a slender tube. Some have a deeper rose-colored throat. They bloom in small clusters at the branch tips. The plant is often used as a ground cover in Hawaii and is virtually everblooming.

Golden Dewdrop
Duranta repens Linnaeus
Verbena family
Tropical America

THE POPULAR name, "golden dewdrop," well describes the clusters of small, bright, orange yellow berries which hang on this shrub a large part of the year. They are so plentiful they usually cause the slender, grey-stemmed branches to droop over gracefully. Flowers and berries often appear at the same time. The flowers are small, in loose clusters, and are either a delicate lavender blue or white. Each has a minute tube and five lobes.

The shrub may grow to eighteen feet but is usually less. It has small, light green leaves, pointed at either end and so plentiful the plant is often used as an informal hedge or screen.

115

Blue Eranthemum

Eranthemum nervosum (Vahl) R. Brown
Acanthus family
India

INTENSELY bright blue flowers, without a touch of lavender in their color, are characteristic of this plant. The truly blue flowers of the world are very limited in number, but this is one of them.

The five small lobes spread from a slender tube whose center holds two yellow stamens. The blossoms appear from a bract which is white with green veins. These bracts, remaining after the flowers fall, form a column which may be several inches long. The plant is a sprawling shrub which may reach six feet. Its leaves are a rough dark green, up to eight inches long.

116

Arnotto or Lipstick Plant
Bixa orellana Linnaeus
Arnotto family
Tropical America

S EED PODS of the arnotto are extremely ornamental and are often used as dried floral material. They are covered with heavy, soft, dark hairs, deep red when fresh and turning to stiff brown as they dry. The pointed pod splits to reveal rows of seeds covered with a red powdery material. This provides the arnotto dye for commercial use formerly used, among other things, for coloring oleomargarine, butter, and cheese. It is not produced commercially in Hawaii, but the plants are grown for ornament.

The dainty flowers are pale orchid pink, the five petals surrounding a central mass of lavender stamens. They bloom in summer. The foliage is dark green and prominently veined. This shrub may attain almost the proportions of a small tree.

White Shrimp Plant
Justicia betonica Linnaeus
Acanthus family
Malaya

THE CONSPICUOUS portions of the inflorescence of this plant are the long spikes, or columns, of green and white bracts, which grow near the branch tips. The spikes are made up of closely packed, heart-shaped leaves, white with green veins. The true flower emerges inconspicuously, here and there, from three of these bract leaves. It is lavender and white with two lips, one with three points, the other with two.

The plant is sprawling, with long, very slender, weak stems. The opposite leaves are long, pointed, with wavy edges and a soft, smooth surface.

Chenille Plant
Acalypha hispida Burmann
Euphorbia family
India

ONE of the most striking of tropical shrubs bears long, thin, velvety tails of dark red, which well deserve the common name of chenille plant. The tails, which may be eighteen inches long, are made up of the staminate flowers which have no petals. The pistillate flowers are inconspicuous. Leaves are a bright green, oblong, pointed, slightly toothed, and four to eight inches long. The shrub will attain eight feet or more.

119

Dwarf Poinciana
Poinciana pulcherrima Linnaeus or
Caesalpinia pulcherrima (L) Swartz
Legume, senna subfamily
Tropical cosmopolitan

BRIGHT clusters of fiery scarlet and yellow flowers growing on the higher branches of a tall shrub or small tree suggest the blossoms of the royal poinciana. Actually, they are close relatives. Individual flowers are smaller, with five thin, spreading petals and a colorful calyx. The petals are sometimes margined with yellow, which adds to the brilliant effect. Conspicuous are long, red stamens and a pistil, which project from the center.

Flat seed pods follow the flowers.

There is an all-yellow form (variety *flava)* which is similar in every respect except color.

The leaves of the plant are of double compound form, with many extremely small leaflets, rounded in outline. The shrub grows widely through the tropics of both Asia and America so that its original home is now uncertain.

Another tree with very similar flowers, but of lighter yellow, can be distinguished easily from the yellow above by the tufts of long, red stamens. This is *Poinciana gilliesii* or *Caesalpinia gilliesii,* sometimes called bird of paradise tree.

Plumbago

Plumbago capensis Thunberg
Leadwort family
South Africa

HEADS of delicate baby blue flowers on a woody, climbing shrub are the plumbago. The plant is composed of numerous long, thin branches, which will pile on one another and mat up into a thick undergrowth with the green growth on top. The plant is used as a ground cover or a hedge, or it may push over rocks or climb part way up a tree.

The flowers appear in small clusters at the branch tips. They are composed of a long, thin tube which opens to five delicate, blue lobes. In spite of their delicacy they are surprisingly strong, so that they have been made into leis. The intensity of the blue color varies considerably, from bright to pale, and there is also a white variety. Sticky hairs cover the short calyx. Leaves are oblong and stemless.

121

Kalamona or
Scrambled Eggs

Cassia glauca Lamarck
Daisy, senna subfamily
Southeastern Asia

A VERY commonly seen shrub or small tree in Hawaii, bearing clusters of bright orange yellow flowers and, at the same time, bunches of brown pods, is called after "Solomon in all his glory." Solomon, rendered into the Hawaiian language becomes Kalamona. The second common name of this plant, "scrambled eggs," is an apt description of the way the clusters of yellow flowers seem to have been dribbled over it. They are practically everblooming. Individual flowers are very similar to those of its cousin, the golden shower tree, with five similar petals. The compound leaves are made up of about eight pairs of oblong leaflets. Clusters of pods are usually a characteristic feature. This shrub is often seen growing wild, especially in rather dry situations.

122

Candle Bush or Acapulco

Cassia alata Linnaeus
Daisy, senna subfamily
Tropical America

UPRIGHT heads of yellow flowers, almost cylindrical in form, suggest candles and give its popular name to this shrub or small tree. The greater part of the cylinder is made up of unopened buds, but a few flowers at a time open at the base. The blooming season is long, but is at its best in winter.

The plant is rather coarse in form, with large luxuriant leaves. They are compound, made up of many pairs of large blunt-tipped leaflets which increase in size from base to tip. The plant is widely grown, often in semiwild places, for it is drought resistant. It will become twelve feet high.

123

Poinsettia
Euphorbia pulcherrima Willdenow
Spurge family
Mexico

VISITORS to Hawaii at holiday time are usually amazed at the brilliance and abundance of these well known flowers, as they grow out of doors in banks and hedges. They also observe that most of those seen are double, with huge shaggy heads of many red leaves. The color of the double variety is deeper and richer than the scarlet of the common single red. If left untrimmed this plant may attain the proportions of a small tree, twelve feet high, but better flowers are obtained by cutting it back once or twice a year.

The poinsettia is a "short day" bloomer, that is, its blooming period is conditioned by the length of time it receives daylight. This accounts for the great regularity of its blooming period in November and December, when the hours of the day are right for its appearance. Cases are known when the blooming period has been postponed by brilliant street lights which prolong the lighted period.

The other varieties of poinsettia sometimes seen are the rose pink and the creamy white. Both are interesting, less brilliant, but more subtle in hue than the rich flag red.

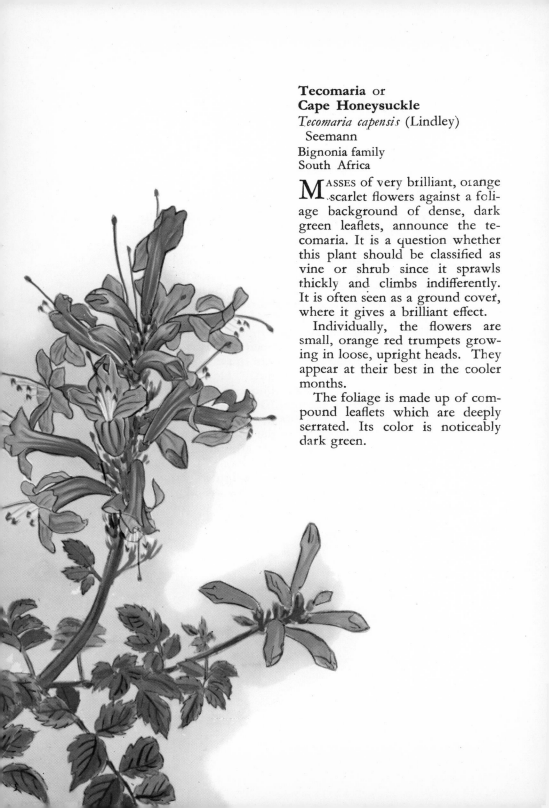

Tecomaria or
Cape Honeysuckle
Tecomaria capensis (Lindley)
  Seemann
Bignonia family
South Africa

MASSES of very brilliant, orange scarlet flowers against a foliage background of dense, dark green leaflets, announce the tecomaria. It is a question whether this plant should be classified as vine or shrub since it sprawls thickly and climbs indifferently. It is often seen as a ground cover, where it gives a brilliant effect.

Individually, the flowers are small, orange red trumpets growing in loose, upright heads. They appear at their best in the cooler months.

The foliage is made up of compound leaflets which are deeply serrated. Its color is noticeably dark green.

Chapter Five

Tropicalia

CERTAIN plants seem to fit the description "tropical" more than do the trees, vines, and shrubs described in other chapters of this book. The words "tropical" and "exotic" bring to mind pictures of large, lush leaves and heavily waxen, strange, and unfamiliar flowers. Some such plants are shown in the following pages. Although few, if any of them demand conditions any more truly tropical than do others, it seems as if they should, just from their strangeness.

All of these plants may be grown outdoors, but greenhouses do exist in the tropics, and certain plants are more successfully grown in them than elsewhere. But these structures usually have only a roof of glass, while side walls are merely of wire screening. The purpose of such greenhouses is to give protection from wind, rain, and insects and to increase moisture in the air. An excellent public greenhouse display of rare and beautiful tropical plants is found in Foster Botanical Garden in Honolulu. This is a public park, open every day except Christmas and New Years day, without charge.

Wild or **Philippine Orchid**

Spathoglottis plicata Blume
Orchid family
Malaya

THIS LITTLE terrestrial orchid has found the climate of Hawaii so congenial it has jumped the garden fence and now grows wild in many places. It is a low plant with narrow, pointed leaves which have thin, lengthwise ridges. Above these rise the flowering stalks with heads of small flowers. Usually they are lavender, but certain varieties, or hybrids, may be pink, white, or yellow. Indi-vidual flowers appear to have five starlike petals, but only two of these are actual petals; three are sepals of almost similar form. The third petal, called the "lip," is quite differently shaped, as with so many orchids. It appears as a curious floral part with three small lobes in the center of the flower and a long, drooping portion, or tongue, which widens at the tip. Seeds, almost dust-fine, form in small, green capsules, about one and a half inches long, which hang from the stem.

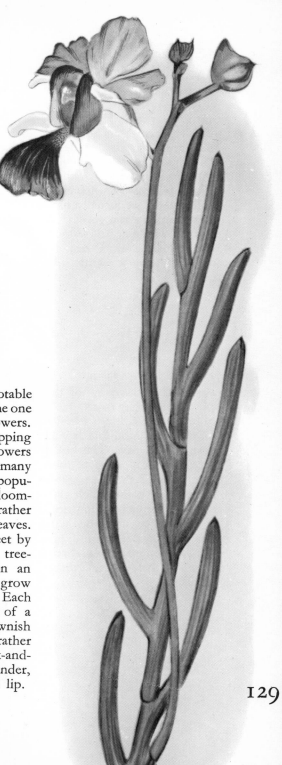

Baby Orchid or
Vanda Miss Joaquim
Vanda teres × *Vanda hookeriana*
Orchid family
Horticultural

THIS HYBRID vanda orchid is notable in Hawaii because it has become one of the most important of the lei flowers. It is also an important item for shipping to the mainland. Commercial growers produce the plants by the acre and many home gardens hold rows. They are popular because they are almost everblooming. The plant has small, rounded, rather succulent stems and cylindrical leaves. An epiphyte, it may climb to six feet by clinging to some material such as treefern trunks. The flowers appear on an upright stalk, which continues to grow and produce buds for a long time. Each flower is about the size and shape of a pansy, lavender in color with a brownish center. Its actual construction is rather complex with a five-parted calyx-and-petal portion, which is light lavender, and a deeper-colored, three-parted lip.

HELICONIAS

Banana family
Tropical America

THESE STRIKING tropical plants, most of them with a dramatic inflorescence, are related to the banana. A few species are short, but most are large, the paddle-shaped leaves of some reaching twenty feet. The inflorescence is made up of a stalk holding a series of highly colored bracts, within which are the true flowers, usually inconspicuous. In spite of the size of the flowering stalks, they are usually hard to see among the leaves, so that the whole flower is more often noticed as a cut decoration than growing in a garden.

Lobster Claw

Heliconia humilis Jacquin

THE COMMON name of this plant derives from a series of bracts, the color of a boiled lobster. Their outline is suggestive of a claw. The bracts grow close together, on alternate sides of the heavy stalk and in one plane. Each claw may be five inches long from stalk to tip, and the stalk three or four feet long. The small, green flowers can hardly be seen inside these brilliant bracts.

THE FLOWERING stalk of this species is quite similar to the lobster claw, opposite, in form, but is differently colored. Each bract is daintily bordered with green and yellow and has a wide, pink cheek. It blooms early in the spring.

Other Heliconias

(not illustrated)

THE HANGING heliconia *(H. collinsiana* Griggs) is one of the most striking flowers seen in Hawaii. It blooms in late summer and autumn. A tall stalk, like a fishpole, six to eight feet high, has a dramatic fall of flowers, drooping and swaying from its upper end. It is made up of a series of pointed keels, pinkish red in color, widely spaced, narrow, but long and pointed. The flowers inside are bright yellow and large enough to be conspicuous. On the plant, even this large flower may be almost concealed, but it makes a wonderful cut decoration.

The golden heliconia *(H. latispatha* Bentham) has a flowering stalk which pushes above the leaves, unlike most of this group. The widely spaced, pointed keels are deep orange yellow in color and quite long and narrow.

Pink and Green Heliconia
Heliconia elongata Griggs

131

132

Bird of Paradise
Strelitzia reginae Banks
Banana family
South Africa

THIS GORGEOUS flower deserves its popular name, for it suggests a bird's head with a great golden crest, topping a long neck. The bird's head and beak is indicated by a pointed sheath, while the crest is formed by flowers rising from it. About six blossoms are packed in the sheath, and one emerges every other day, so the cluster grows larger and brighter as it becomes older. Each flower has three pointed petals, brilliantly orange in color, and a central, blue, arrow-shaped portion. This is a modified stamen, known as a staminodium.

The banana-like plant is made up of a clump of stiff, paddle-shaped leaves growing on strong, greyish stems each from two to five feet high. The leaf blade is thick and heavy, with parallel venation, and the edges curve inward. The underside is covered with a greyish, waxen bloom, and on young leaves the midrib is red.

White Bird of Paradise
Strelitzia nicolai Regel and
  Koernicke
Banana family
South Africa
(no illustration)

THE "WHITE BIRD" is the flower of a tree which has large, banana-like leaves growing in a single plane, like the sticks of a fan. Several such fans usually make up a single tree. The flowering stalk pushes out from among these leaves, but it is very short and so the blossoms are often not easily seen from the ground. Each flowering stalk holds two or three pointed sheaths, brownish in color, pointing in different directions. From these the flowers break out, each with three white petals. An arrow-shaped, blue portion is similar to the one in the golden bird of paradise. The general effect of this inflorescence does not suggest a bird's head, as does the one above, because of the several sheaths and the lack of a long stem. It makes a very striking flower arrangement when cut.

133

GINGER BLOSSOMS

LEADING among Hawaii's special flowers are the gingers. The name covers several groups which vary considerably in appearance, but the similarities which relate them can usually be noted easily. They are not far removed, botanically, from the cannas and the bananas, hence they are reedlike plants with fibrous stalks and blade-shaped leaves. Some are short, hardly more than a ground cover, others grow to twelve or fifteen feet in height. A native Hawaiian ginger, called awapuhi, is *Zingiber zerumbet*. It grows wild in the Hawaiian forests, the leaves forming a ground cover a foot or two high. In spring the flower heads spring up, bulbous and reddish, composed of scaly bracts, out of which appear the small, inconspicuous, yellowish flowers. The plant from whose root is made the dried ginger of gingerbread also grows in Hawaii. It is called Chinese ginger or *Zingiber officinale*. Its light-skinned rootstalk is also made into candied and preserved ginger, and bits of the fresh root, or young shoot, often add piquancy to island cooking.

Red Ginger
Alpinia purpurata (Vieillard) K. Schumann
Ginger family
East Indies
(opposite, left)

A CONSPICUOUS upright head of rich, rosy crimson bloom among rich green foliage marks the red ginger flower. This floral head, growing at the end of the leafstalk, may be a foot or more long. It is made up of red bracts rather thick, large, and open, which could be mistaken for petals. The true flowers, small, white, and tubular, emerge here and there from the base of the bracts. As the inflorescence matures it elongates, and small, green-leaved adventitious plantlets appear between the bracts, mingling their green with the red. If the head finally bends over to the ground, these take root. The long, lush leafstalks rise from the ground sometimes to eight feet. They carry strong, leathery leaf blades, often over two feet in length. This plant is everblooming.

Shell Ginger

Alpinia nutans (Andres) Roscoe
Ginger family
Tropical East Asia
(previous illustration, right)

LIKE A STIFF strand of closely strung shells, the buds of this ginger droop in a cluster from the ends of the leafstalks. Each bud has a thin porcelain-like texture and is white, tipped in bright pink. The buds open one or two at a time, and the flower pushes out. It has thin, white petals, while a larger ruffled portion is yellow, marked with red, veinlike lines. Sometimes the flowers mature into small, golden balls, which make ornamental cut arrangements. The plant is made up of long stalks, up to twelve feet high, which carry luxuriant, alternate leaf blades. The blades are long and pointed, about five inches wide and up to two feet long.

Crepe or Malay Ginger

Costus speciosus (Koenig) Smith
Ginger family
East Indies

RUFFLED and fringed white flowers of odd form emerge, two or three at a time, from behind the scales of the large, brownish red bracts of the costus. These bracts form a dark head, often so large as to suggest a small pineapple. The white flowers have a curious structure. The three true petals are white and rather inconspicuous behind a large, crepy, white portion, which seems to be the petal but is really a greatly modified stamen, called a staminodium. This rolls into a bell form, with fringed and fluted edges and a pale yellow throat. A second, modified stamen carries the anthers and has a yellow tip, making it appear like the usual center of a flower. The stems of this plant have a tendency to curve spirally. The leaves are not so long and bladelike as in other gingers and are arranged spirally on the stem.

138

White Ginger or
Ginger Lily

Hedychium coronarium Koenig
Ginger family
India

MOST ROMANTIC of all the gingers, because of its ethereal delicacy and enchanting fragrance is the blossom of the white ginger. The petals are moon-white, with a shimmering crystalline quality. They are shaped like a moth, with a pair of petals resembling wings and a third like folded wings, while a slender filament in the center is like a moth's antennae.

The flower head at the end of the leaf stem is a smooth, waxen, green bulb made of scalelike bracts. Behind each scale is a flower, several of which push out at the same time.

The plant is made up of strong, fibrous leaf stems coming from the ground sometimes to a height of seven feet. They hold large, blade-shaped leaflets.

Torch Ginger

Phaeomeria magnifica (ROSCOE)
  K. Schumann
Ginger family
Indonesia
(see next page for illustration)

THIS IS the most magnificent of the gingers and one of the most spectacular flowers in the world. The general form of the blossom is that of the classical, conventionalized torch, a waxen cone, either pink or red, surrounded by a frill-like involucre. This head, which may be as much as ten inches across, grows at the end of a long stalk that rises directly from the ground. It usually emerges several inches from the nearest leafstalk. The cone is made up of innumerable waxy bracts, laid in scalelike formation. The red variety has its bracts edged in white. The frill is made of much larger bracts in solid color. From behind these bracts push out the small, yellow, true flowers. They rather spoil the symmetry of the cone, which is most attractive before they appear.

The plant is made up of large, sparse, canelike stalks, sometimes twenty feet high. Each stalk holds alternate leaf blades, pointed and up to two feet or more long.

140

Yellow Ginger
Hedychium flavum Roxburgh
Ginger family
India

THE YELLOW ginger has flowers like slender moths of pale creamy yellow. They rise at the end of narrow tubes above a green head composed of scaly bracts. One blossom emerges from behind each scale, and the buds of those above it peep out like yellow quills. The flower has three petals, two paired and winglike, the third large and looking like a second pair of wings, folded together There are three slender sepals and a long filament of deeper color, holding the pistil and stamen. The blossoms have a delicate fragrance, delightful when perfectly fresh, but a little rank when the least bit wilted. Leaves are blade-shaped and luxuriant. The flowers are used to make a traditional lei, one of the most widespread in the Pacific.

141

Anthurium or
Flamingo Flower

Authurium andraeanum Lindley
Arum family
Colombia

THE STRIKING flower of the anthurium is made up of a finger-like spike, white, pinkish, or yellow, encircled by a colored bract that is heart-shaped. Its colors range from pure white through all shades of pink to deep, rich red. The latter is the preferred color because of its brilliance. The flower is very popular for cut purposes since it often lasts three weeks. Its waxen quality is so pronounced it is sometimes taken to be artificial. The true flowers are found on the spike, very tiny and packed tightly together so that they are often unnoticed. When fertilized they may turn into berries like warts, on the spike. The waxen bract sometimes turns green, showing that it is really a modified leaf.

The plant has a short central stalk from which grow the long-stemmed, heart-shaped leaves. The size of the flowers depends on the size of the leaves and plant, the larger the leaves the larger the flowers. The whole plant may become two feet high.

A smaller flower that is quite similar, but has the central spike curled is called the pigtail anthurium, botanically *Anthurium scherzerianum*.

Kahili Ginger

Hedychium gardnerianum Roscoe
Ginger family
Himalayas
(no illustration)

THE LOCAL name for this ginger is derived from the *kahili*, an item that was part of the regalia of early Hawaiian chieftains. A kahili was made from a pole or wand, near the top of which, and at right angles to it, were affixed long, wing or tail feathers from certain large birds, forming a cylindrical head. This was carried, like a banner, wherever the chief went, to announce his rank and presence.

The blossoming head of the ginger called after the kahili shows an obvious resemblance. The small, yellow flowers on long, stemlike tubes form a cylinder around the top of the stalk, while the resemblance to feathers is enhanced by long, red filaments which are very striking against the yellow of the petals. Individual flowers have the general form of the yellow ginger, but are much smaller and their color is not creamy, but bright yellow. The flower stalks may be six feet long and rise above the rest of the plant.

142

143

Spathiphyllum

Spathiphyllum species, var. *cleve-landii* (probably derived from *S. kochii*)

Arum family
Horticultural

FREQUENTLY seen as a ground cover in shady Honolulu gardens is an attractive plant, about eighteen inches high, with flowers somewhat like a small, white calla . The white bract, however, is thin, flat, and delicately waxen, instead of parchment-like as in the calla. The spike is white and rough, instead of golden. This spike is made up of the true flowers, its roughness being due to the massed pistils. The plant grows as a clump of attractive leaves, long, narrow, wavy-edged, and with prominent venation. The flowers rise above the foliage on stalks growing through a leaf stem.

The derivation and specific name of this plant is not certain. It is generally called *S. clevelandii,* a name not found in botanical plant lists.

The spathiphyllum groups come mostly from tropical America.

Fragrant Spathiphyllum

Spathiphyllum species
  (probably derived from
  S. cannaefolium)
Arum family
Horticultural

THE WHITE bract of this calla-like flower is flat and greenish beneath and rather thick in texture. The spike is smooth and greenish. The flower has a slight but pleasant fragrance. Leaves are pointed ovals, rather dull green, on short stems.

McCoy Hybrid Spathiphyllum
(no illustration)

THIS IS a very large plant, leaves being sometimes three feet long. Flowers are greenish white, with a rough, white spike.

145

Common Ape

Xanthosoma roseum Schott
Arum family
Central America

THE WORD *"ape"* (pronounced ah-pay) is applied in Hawaii to a large number of plants, all of them with the "elephant ear" type of leaf. The leaves are arrowhead- or heart-shaped and the flowers are of the jack-in-the-pulpit or calla form. The common ape, while not the largest of this group, has huge leaves about three feet long and half as wide. They grow on long stems which rise from a short, thick trunk. The leaves are dull green and somewhat powdery beneath.

The flowers are usually hidden by these large leaves although each blossom is six to eight inches long. The inflorescence rises on a thick stalk near the top of the trunk. It consists of a pinkish, hoodlike bract enwrapping a thick spike. On the spike are the true flowers, very minute and almost invisible. The bract is constricted somewhat below its center. The flower has a rank, rather unpleasant smell.

This plant is closely related to the taros, which resemble it in general form but are smaller. There are many varieties of taro, the heavy rootstalk of which serves as a food for Pacific and south Asian peoples. In Hawaii it is boiled, peeled, and mashed to a paste and called poi.

Nightblooming Cereus
Hylocereus undatus (Haw.) Britt and Rose
Cactus family
Mexico

ONE OF Hawaii's most famous flowers is, strangely enough, a Mexican cactus. It was brought here directly from Acapulco by a sea captain in the early days and presented to a missionary teacher. She planted it on the Punahou campus where it has been growing ever since as a hedge. On the nights when it blooms, this hedge becomes a mecca for hundreds of visitors. The nightblooming cereus, as romantic as its name, opens its great buds about eight o'clock in the evening at periodic intervals between June and October. There are ten days to two weeks between these outbursts of bloom. The plant is a climber·with fleshy, three-sided stems, their edges scalloped and spiny. It will push these thick stems up walls and banks or even high into trees, sometimes for a length of sixty feet.

Small buds appear along the stems for the first time about the middle of June. They increase rapidly in size until they are almost a foot long, egg-shaped, and enclosed in greenish yellow sepals. A few may open on preliminary evenings, but most will open together on the same night. The movement of the sepals and petals is fast enough to be perceptible. They unfold to form a deep, scentless cup, which is filled with many pale gold stamens. The style hangs among them. The flowers remain open until the heat of morning wilts them and they droop and close.

Pineapple Lily

Billbergia thyrsoidea Martius
Pineapple family
Brazil

MANY MEMBERS of the pineapple family have striking and unusual flowers, but none is more brilliant than this one. The plant is a low rosette of tough, green leaves. They are strap-shaped, about two feet long, and have spiny edges. From the center of this rosette pushes out a dense blossom head on a short, fleshy white stem. The head is made up of small, powdery, stemless, pinkish red flowers. Each has three small curving petals and a tuft of yellow stamens, while the pistil has a blue tip. The short, white blossom stem carries numerous pink, ribbon-like bracts.

Ligularia,
Leopard Plant, or **Farfugium**
Ligularia kaempferi Siebold and
  Zuccarini
Daisy family
Japan

THIS LITTLE plant, about a foot high, is grown in shady Hawaiian gardens mostly as a ground cover. It is very attractive with its luxuriant, rounded, glossy leaves. They are about six inches across and indented where the leaf stem is attached. The clumps rise from underground stems. Sometimes, when the leaves are spotted with white or yellow, it is called leopard plant. Stalks of small, yellow flowers occasionally push above the leaves. The flowers are like single daisies. Later, like dandelions, they develop into a tuft of fluffy hairs.

151

Zephyr Flower

Zephyranthes candida Herbert
Amaryllis family
Argentine

THIS IS a small, bulbous border plant with grasslike leaves which are less than a foot long. Small, white flowers suggest a crocus, each on an individual stem. They have six white petals which are sometimes a little rose-colored on the outside. The center of the flower holds golden anthers and a stigma, which is slightly three-lobed.

In temperate climates, this South American plant sends up its leaves and flowers in the fall. In Hawaii it is always green and may bloom at any time.

Index

Acacia koa, 18
Acalypha
  hispida, 119
  wilkesiana, 100
Acapulco, 123
African tulip tree, 22
Aleurites moluccana, 12
Allamanda cathartica, 86
Aloe ciliaris, 104
Alpinia
  nutans, 136
  purpurata, 134
Alyxia olivaeformis, 14
Angel's trumpet, 31
Anthurium
  andraeanum, 142
  scherzerianum, 142
  pigtail, 142
Antigonon leptopus, 81
Ape, common, 146
Ardisia solanacea, 39
Argyroxiphium sandwicense, 7
Arnotto, 117
Artocarpus incisus, 17
Awapuhi, 134

Bag flower, 64
Bagnit, 72
Bamboo, introduction of, 2
Banana, introduction of, 2
Bauhinia
  corymbosa, 69
  galpini, 103
  monandra, 33
  red, 103
  variegata, 26

Beach naupaka, 7, 18
Beaumontia jerdoniana, 71
Beefsteak plant, 100
Beloperone guttata, 105
Bengal trumpet, 57
Be-still tree, 38
Bignonia
  magnifica, 62
  purple, 62
  unguis-cati, 65
  venusta, 77
Billbergia thyrsoidea, 150
Bird of paradise, 133
  tree, 120
  white, 133
Bixa orellana, 117
"Black-eyed susan," 56
Bleeding heart, 64
Blue sky flower, 57
Bombax ellipticum, 27
Bottle brush tree, 46
Bougainvillea
  glabra, 85
  var. sanderiana, 85
  spectabilis, 85
  spectabilis var. lateritia, 85
  spectabilis var. parviflora, 85
Bower plant, 75
Brassaia actinophylla, 54
Brazilian glory, 73
Brazilian golden vine, 68
Breadfruit tree, 17
  introduction of, 2
Brunfelsia
  americana, 92
  latifolia, 92

Buttercup tree, 47
Butterfly hibiscus, 89
Butterfly pea, 76

Cadeña de amor, 81
Caesalpinia
  gilliesii, 120
  pulcherrima, 120
Calliandra inaequilatera, 93
Callistemon lanceolatus, 46
Calophyllum inophyllum, 17
Calotropis gigantea, 98
Canavalia microcarpa, 79
Candle bush, 123
Candlenut tree, 12
  introduction of, 2
Cannon ball tree, 37
Carissa grandiflora, 91
Cassia
  alata, 123
  fistula, 51
  glauca, 122
  grandis, 49
  hybrida, 51
  javanica, 48
Cat's claw climber, 65
Cereus, nightblooming, 148
Ceylon morning-glory, 82
Chain of love, 81
Champak
  orange, 42
  white, 42
Chenille plant, 119
Chinese star jasmine, 61
Chinese hibiscus, 89
Christmas
  cosmos, 112
  daisy, 112
Christmas berry tree, 30
Clerodendron
  fragrans, 102
  thomsonae, 64
Climbing lily, 70
Clitoria ternatea, 76

Cochlospermum
  hibiscoides, 47
  vitifolium, 47
Coconut, 9
  introduction of, 2
Cocos nucifera, 9
Codiaeum variegatum, 96
Colvillea racemosa, 28
Confederate jasmine, 61
Copper leaf, 100
Coral hibiscus, 89
Coral shower tree, 49
Corallita, 81
Cordia
  sebestena, 43
  subcordata, 43
Cordyline terminalis, 19
Costus speciosus, 136
Couroupita guianensis, 37
Crepe ginger, 136
Crepe myrtle tree, 29
Croton, 96
Crown flower, 98
Crown of thorns, 109
Cup of gold, 63
Cydista aequinoctialis, 66

Datura candida, 31
Delonix regia, 24
Dombeya wallichii, 23
Doxanthus unguis-cati, 65
Duranta repens, 115

Endemism in Hawaii, 5
Equinox vine, 66
Eranthemum
  blue, 116
  golden, 107
  nervosum, 116
Erythrina
  indica, 45
  monosperma, 45
  sandwicensis, 45
  variegata, 45

154

Eugenia
  jambos, 40
  malaccensis, 13
Euphorbia
  pulcherrima, 125
  splendens, 109

Farfugium, 151
Fern
  introduction of, 4
  tree, use of, 7
Flamboyant, 24
Flamingo flower, 142
Forty-ninth state, official flower
  of, 11
Foster Botanical Garden, 37, 127
Frangipani, 53

Galphimia
  glauca, 101
  vine, 72
Gardenia taitensis, 111
Garlic-scented vine, 66
Geiger tree, 43
Geology of Hawaii, 1
Ginger
  Chinese, 134
  crepe, 136
  flowers, 134
  Hawaiian, 134
  kahili, 142
  lily, 139
  Malay, 136
  red, 134
  shell, 136
  torch, 139
  white, 139
  wild, introduction of, 3
  yellow, 7, 141
Gliricidia sepium, 36
Gloriosa lily, 70
Gloriosa rothschildiana, 70
Gold tree, 44
Golden dewdrop, 115

Golden shower tree, 51
Gourd, bottle, introduction of, 3

Hala, 10
Hau tree, 16
  introduction of, 2
  use of, 7
Hawaii National Park, 7, 15
Hedychium
  coronarium, 139
  flavum, 141
  gardnerianum, 142
Heliconia
  collinsiana, 131
  elongata, 131
  golden, 131
  humilis, 130
  latispatha, 131
  pink and green, 131
Heliconias, general, 130
Hibiscus, 87
  arnottianus, 87
  butterfly, 89
  Chinese, 89
  common red, 89
  coral, 89
  hybrids, 89
  native Hawaiian white, 87
  rosa-sinensis, 89
  schizopetalus, 89
  tiliaceus, 16
  waterfall, 89
  yellow, 89
Hinano, 10
Honeysuckle
  cape, 126
  pink, 94
Hoya carnosa, 67
Huapala, 77
Hug-me-tight, 65
Hylocereus undatus, 148

Ilima, 11
  as lei flower, 7

Indian coral tree, 45
Indigenous plants of Hawaii, 5
Ipomoea
  horsfalliae, 73
  tuberosa, 82
Ixora
  macrothyrsa, 99
  odorata, 99

Jacaranda ovalifolia, 34
Jade vine, 60
Jasmine, confederate, 61
Jasmine tea, 59
Jasminum
  pubescens, 58, 61
  sambac, 59
Jetberry tree, 39
Justicia
  betonica, 118
  coccinea, 90

Kahili ginger, 142
Kalamona, 122
Kamani tree, 17
Kigelia pinnata, 41
Koa tree, 18
Koki'o, 87
Kou
  use of, 7
  wood, 43
Kou haole, 43
Kuhio vine, 73
Kukui tree, 12
  introduction of, 2

Lady of the night, 92
Lagerstroemia speciosa, 29
Lantana
  camara, 110
  sellowiana, 110
  trailing, 110
Lasiandra, 106
Lauhala, 10
Lehua flower, 7, 15

Lehua haole, 93
Leis, early Hawaiian, 6
Leopard plant, 151
Ligularia kaempferi, 151
Lipstick plant, 117
Lobster claw, 130
Lochnera rosea, 114
Lonicera heckrottii, 94

Madagascar periwinkle, 114
Madre de cacao, 36
Maile, 14
Malay apple, 13
Malay ginger, 136
Malpighia coccigera, 108
Mauna loa vine, 79
Melia, 53
Metrosideros collina, 15
Mexican creeper, 81
Michelia
  alba, 42
  champaca, 42
Milkweed, giant Indian, 98
Milo tree, 17
  introduction of, 3
  use of, 7
Montanoa hibiscifolia, 112
Mountain apple, 13
Mulberry, paper, introduction
  of, 3

Natal plum, 91
Naupaka, beach, 7, 18
Nerium
  indicum, 95
  oleander, 95
Nightblooming cereus, 148

Octopus, 54
Odontonema strictum, 90
Ohia lehua, 15, 93
Oleander, 95
Oleander, yellow, 38
Orange trumpet, 77

Orchid
  baby, 129
  Philippine, 128
  vanda, 129
  vine, 68
  wild, 128
Orchid tree, 26

Pak-lan, 42
Pandanus odoratissimus, 10
Pandorea
  brycei, 75
  jasminoides, 75
Pedilanthus tithymaloides, 113
Peltophorum inerme, 25
Pepper tree, California, 30
Petrea volubilis, 80
Phaeomeria magnifica, 139
Phanera, 69
Pigtail anthurium, 142
Pikake, 59
Pineapple lily, 150
Pink and white shower tree, 48
Plant introductions, 1
Plumbago capensis, 121
Plumeria
  acutifolia, 53
  obtusa, 53
  rubra, 53
  Singapore, 53
Poi, 146
Poinciana
  dwarf, 120
  gilliesii, 120
  pulcherrima, 120
  red, 24
  royal, 24
  yellow, 25
Poinsettia, 125
Porana paniculata, 78
Porana vine, 78
Potato tree, 32
Primavera, 44
Prince's vine, 73

Pseuderanthemum reticulatum, 107
Pudding-pipe tree, 51
Pumeli, 53
Purple allamanda, 56
Purple bignonia, 62
Pyrostegia ignea, 77

Rain of gold, 101
Rainbow bougainvillea, 85
Rainbow shower tree, 51
Red justicia, 90
Rosa de montaña, 81
Rose apple, 40
Royal poinciana, 24

St. Thomas tree, 33
Sandpaper vine, 80
Sausage tree, 41
Scaevola frutescens, 18
Scented star jasmine, 58
Schinus terebinthifolius, 30
Scrambled eggs, 122
Screwpine, 10
Shell ginger, 136
Shower
  coral, 49
  golden, 50
  pink and white, 48
  rainbow, 51
Shower trees, blooming period, 21
Shrimp plant, 105
  white, 118
Sida fallax, 11
Silver cup, 63
Silver sword, 7
Singapore holly, 108
Singapore plumeria, 53
Slipper flower, 113
Snow creeper, 78
Solandra
  grandiflora, 63
  guttata, 63

157

Solanum macranthum, 32
Spanish arbor vine, 82
Spathiphyllum
    cannaefolium, 145
    clevelandii, 144
    fragrant, 145
    kochii, 144
    McCoy hybrid, 145
Spathodea campanulata, 22
Spathoglottis plicata, 128
Species, origin of, in Hawaii, 5
Stephanotis floribunda, 74
Stigmatophyllum
    ciliatum, 68
    littorale, 68
Strelitzia
    nicolai, 133
    reginae, 133
Strongylodon macrobotrys, 60
Sugar cane, introduction of, 3
Sweet potato, introduction of, 3

Tabebuia
    donnell-smithii, 44
    pentaphylla, 35
Tahitian gardenia, 111
Taro, introduction of, 3
Taros, 146
Tecoma pentaphylla, 35
Tecomaria capensis, 126
Thespesia populnea, 17
Thevetia
    nereifolia, 38
    peruviana, 38
Thunbergia
    alata, 56
    bush, 97
    erecta, 97
    fragrans, 56
    grandiflora, 57
    large-flowered, 57
    lauvel-leaved, 56
    laurifolia, 56
Ti, colored, 20

Ti plant, 19, 20
    introduction of, 3
Tiare, 111
Tibouchina semidecandra, 106
Tiger's claw, 45
Torch ginger, 139
Trachelospermum   jasminoides,
    58, 61
Trailing lantana, 110
Tristellateia australasiae, 72
Tropicalia, 127
Thryallis glauca, 101

Umbrella tree, 54

Vanda
    hookeriana, 129
    Miss Joaquim, 129
    orchid, 129
    teres, 129
Vinca rosea, 114

Wardian cases, 2
Wax vine, 67
White ginger, 139
White thunbergia, 57
Wilder, Gerrit, plumeria, 53
Wili-wili tree, 45
Wood rose, 82

Xanthosoma roseum, 146

Yam, introduction of, 3
Yellow allamanda, 86
Yellow ginger, 141
    for leis, 7
"Yesterday-today-and-tomor-
    row," 92

Zephyr flower, 152
Zephyranthes candida, 152
Zingiber
    officinale, 134
    zerumbet, 134